FACING
THE
FORCES
OF
CHANGE®

Lead
the Way
in the
Supply
Chain

N·A·W
Institute for
DISTRIBUTION
EXCELLENCE

PEMBROKE
CONSULTING

About NAW and the NAW Institute for Distribution Excellence

The National Association of Wholesaler-Distributors (NAW) was created in 1946 to deal with issues of interest to the entire merchant wholesale distribution industry, thereby freeing affiliated associations to concentrate on the concerns specific to their lines of trade. NAW is a federation of more than 100 wholesale distribution associations and thousands of individual firms that collectively total more than 40,000 companies.

The role of the NAW Institute for Distribution Excellence (formerly the Distribution Research and Education Foundation) is to sponsor and disseminate research into strategic management issues affecting the wholesale distribution industry. The NAW Institute for Distribution Excellence aims to help merchant wholesaler-distributors remain the most effective and efficient channel in distribution.

ISBN 1-934014-00-1

NAW Institute for Distribution Excellence
1725 K Street, NW, Suite 300
Washington, DC 20006
202.872.0885
www.nawpubs.org

Contents

Acknowledgments

The NAW Institute for Distribution Excellence and Pembroke Consulting thank the more than 1,300 individuals who gave considerable time and effort to participate in our online surveys. It is a tribute to the industry that so many talented individuals were willing to share their experiences and opinions to the benefit of all.

We are particularly grateful to the following people who shared their time with the research team via personal interviews, in-depth conversations, or detailed responses to survey questions:

- Julian Archer, Lawson Software
- Dan Casey, Stanion Wholesale Electric Co.
- Julie Copeland, Arbill Safety Products
- Ted Cowie, Safety Today
- John D'Amaro, H.D. Smith Wholesale Drug Company
- Gary Daniels, Johnstone Supply
- Tim Dewey, Delaware Valley Wholesale Florist
- Patrick Dussinger, Interline Brands
- Georgia Dutro, D&D Tool & Supply
- Rick Fine, Duncan Supply Company, Inc.
- Tom Gale, Gale Media
- Gary Glanzman, Eastway Supplies, Inc.
- Michael Glenn, U.S. Bureau of Economic Analysis
- John Groot, The Knotts Company Inc.
- Glenn Hart, OREPAC Building Products
- Jack Healey, Industrial Distribution Group Inc.

- Tim Hilton, Carolina Holdings Inc.
- Kevin Hollinger, C.H. Briggs Hardware Co.
- Chris Holt, UPS Supply Chain Solutions
- Tom Jones, Bryan Equipment Sales, Inc.
- Allan Keck, R.W. Smith & Co.
- Donald Kellermeyer, Kellermeyer Company
- Fred Kfoury, Central Paper Products Co.
- Julia Klein, C.H. Briggs Hardware Co.
- Mark Kramer, Laird Plastics, Inc.
- Henry Landes, Delaware Valley Family Business Center
- Andrew Larson, Gustave A. Larson Company
- Don Latham, Canadian Bearings Ltd.
- Christopher R. Lynch, Reid and Wright, Inc.
- Lillian Marsh, IBM Corporation
- John McGrory, Edge Dynamics, Inc.
- Donald McNeeley, Chicago Tube & Iron Co.
- Michael Medart, Medart Inc.
- James C. Miller, Vetus Partners
- David Muhlendorf, Paper and Chemical Supply Co.
- Robin Mullen, AFFLINK Business Solutions
- Steve Nielson, Activus Healthcare Solutions
- Dave Reder, OKI Systems Limited
- Mike Rioux, IDEA Integration Corp.
- Bill Sanford, Interline Brands
- Mark Seitz, Eli Lilly and Company
- Don Sherow, Modern Group Ltd.
- Ed Sleeman, Colorado Drywall Supply
- Dale Smith, H.D. Smith Wholesale Drug Company
- Paul St. Germain, IBM Corporation
- Stewart Strauss, Strauss Paper Company, Inc.
- Stanley I. Sunshine, Stag-Parkway, Inc.
- John Trimble, U.S. Census Bureau
- Kevin Van Dyke, Skinner Nurseries
- Ian Wahlers, Lawson Software
- John Scott Wilkins, Delaware Valley Wholesale Florist
- Ken Wilkins, Delaware Valley Wholesale Florist
- Douglas York, Ewing Irrigation Products
- James York, U.S. Bureau of Labor Statistics
- Steve Yost, The Rowland Company

We are also grateful to our consulting clients for sharpening our thinking and providing us with opportunities to put our ideas into practice. All errors and misinterpretations remain our responsibility.

The following NAW Institute for Distribution Excellence Board Members and Officers deserve credit for the direction they provided during this project:

2007 NAW INSTITUTE FOR DISTRIBUTION EXCELLENCE BOARD OF DIRECTORS AND OFFICERS

Byron Potter, *Chairman*
Dallas Wholesale Builders Supply Inc.

Don Frendberg, *Vice Chairman*
Heating, Airconditioning and Refrigeration Distributors International

Mark Allen
International Foodservice Distributors Association
Andrew Berlin
Berlin Packaging
Dan Blaylock
Adams-Burch Inc.
Inge Calderon
American Supply Association
Charles Cohen
Benco Dental Co.
John Garfinkel
International Sanitary Supply Association
David Griffith
Modern Group Ltd.
Tim Holt
National School Supply and Equipment Association
Julia Klein
C.H. Briggs Company

Mark Kramer
Laird Plastics, Inc.
Andre Lacy
L.D.I. Ltd.
Richard McCarten
Electro-Federation Canada Inc.
Bob Roberts
Roberts Oxygen Company, Inc.
Raymon A. York
Ewing Irrigation Products

●   ●   ●

George Keeley, *Secretary*
Keeley, Kuenn and Reid

Ron Schreibman, *Executive Director*
National Association of Wholesaler-Distributors

Dirk Van Dongen, *President and Treasurer*
National Association of Wholesaler-Distributors

About the Author

Adam J. Fein, Ph.D., conceptualized, researched, and wrote *Facing the Forces of Change®: Lead the Way in the Supply Chain* along with the staff of Pembroke Consulting, Inc.

Dr. Fein is the founder and president of Philadelphia-based Pembroke Consulting. He consults with manufacturers on channel strategy, assists distributors with industry analysis and planning, and advises technology companies on marketing strategy. He is also a popular and provocative keynote speaker for executive planning sessions and industry meetings around the world.

In addition to his consulting work, Dr. Fein conducts independent economic research on the wholesale distribution industry. He has published nearly 100 academic and industry articles, as well as authored or edited seven books for the National Association of Wholesaler-Distributors, including the last two editions of *Facing the Forces of Change®*. Dr. Fein serves as the first Fellow of the NAW Institute for Distribution Excellence (formerly the Distribution Research and Education Foundation) and as a Senior Fellow at The Wharton School of Business' Mack Center for Technological Innovation.

To learn more about Pembroke Consulting, please contact:
Adam J. Fein, Ph.D.
Pembroke Consulting, Inc.
1515 Market Street, Suite 1520
Philadelphia, PA 19102
Phone: 215.523.5700
Web site: www.PembrokeConsulting.com

Foreword

It is my sincere pleasure to present to you our newest *Facing the Forces of Change*®
report, the eighth in an important series that began in 1982. As we continue to report
noteworthy changes occurring in wholesale distribution, we must also announce
a recent change within the organization that publishes these valuable reports.

The Board and I are pleased to announce an historic transformation of the NAW
Distribution Research and Education Foundation (DREF). DREF will now be
known as the NAW Institute for Distribution Excellence. This new NAW Institute
aspires to carry on the distinguished 40-year history of DREF, while broadening
and deepening its mission to produce thoughtful, forward-looking, and educational
offerings for the industry, and deliver them to you in a practical and contemporary
manner. This publication is the beginning of many projects we have planned for this
year and beyond. As always, we welcome your suggestions on areas of research and
product formats that would be meaningful and useful to you and your organization.

Facing the Forces of Change®: *Lead the Way in the Supply Chain* delineates four
major trends that will dominate wholesale distribution's agenda for at least the next
5 years. I believe these issues will impact distribution companies of all sizes and in
all lines of trade. I found the research to be very practical, and the questions for
management discussion and action ideas will help me stimulate discussion among
my own executive team.

In addition, there are chapters that address the specific needs of wholesaler-
distributors serving three critical markets: construction, industrial and commercial,
and retail. And a special chapter discusses trends that are not yet fully formed, but
appear to be emerging.

In producing this latest *Facing the Forces of Change* report, Adam J. Fein and his exceptional staff at Pembroke Consulting have drawn from an impressive data set including in-depth executive interviews, a large survey sample, and many real-world examples. I am also impressed to see that the report provides comparative data from previous reports, a first for the *Facing the Forces of Change* series.

I encourage you to use this report just as we have used its seven predecessors. Read it carefully, think deeply about the business issues it raises, and discuss these issues candidly with your company colleagues. I wish you great success in creating your own plan to lead the way in your supply chain.

Byron Potter
Chairman
NAW Institute for Distribution Excellence
March 2007

Introduction

A new breed of wholesaler-distributors is emerging. These companies are building deep relationships with customers based on an understanding of the true value created by their services and activities. They are charging customers for new services rather than giving away value-added services for free and hoping to recoup the costs with product margins. These wholesaler-distributors build clout with suppliers through superior performance rather than just through sheer size or volume.

The executives running the new breed of wholesale distribution companies recognize that innovation—the development and adoption of new services, new business practices, and new ways of adding value—is the cornerstone of their success. They are continually searching for new ways of generating revenue and profit. They are positioning their companies to lead the supply chain by combining an understanding of their customers' purchasing priorities with a realistic perspective on their best suppliers' business requirements. A distribution executive at an HVAC wholesaler-distributor exemplified this perspective with this comment: "Margins don't erode due to competitive pressure; they erode through lack of attention to the customers' needs and expectations."

The companies and examples described in *Facing the Forces of Change®: Lead the Way in the Supply Chain* are not larger or luckier than their wholesale distribution competitors. Instead, the executives running these companies are doing a better job of positioning their companies in the common external environment faced by all wholesaler-distributors. The difference between the winners and the losers in the future will derive from the ability to link a fundamental understanding of external business trends with an awareness of how to profit from the trends, followed by appropriate strategy execution to deliver results.

Throughout this report, we use the term *supply chain* when describing the sourcing, purchasing, and physical distribution systems that customers use to acquire products. In other words, supply chain analysis takes the perspective of the downstream customer looking upstream at its sources of supply. A customer's supply chain represents a set of functions that can be performed to varying degrees by many different types of organizations: manufacturers, distributors, customers, third-party logistics companies, online companies, etc. This report focuses on improvement and evolution by wholesaler-distributors within the supply chain of their customers.

Our research and experience suggest that the gap between these leading companies and their competitors will widen in the future. This report describes not only major trends facing wholesaler-distributors, but also the innovative strategies and tactics successful distributors are using to generate new opportunities in response to these trends.

The inertia of customer relationships in business-to-business markets continues to sustain wholesaler-distributors that do not respond to external trends. However, the laggards typically operate at lower levels of profitability and have below-market growth rates. This report should serve as a wake-up call for wholesale distribution executives who fail to consider their companies' longer-term strategies. The world is changing, and wholesaler-distributors must keep evolving in order to stay relevant in their respective industry's supply chain. Successful companies also realize that there is never a final, specific end point to strategy because customers and their needs will always be changing. Wholesaler-distributors must have plans to stay abreast of this ever-evolving world.

SEEING THE BIG PICTURE

Leadership in the supply chain also means accepting the realities of the market, while simultaneously identifying creative solutions to these realities. Many of the trends introduced in our 2004 report *Facing the Forces of Change®: The Road to Opportunity* are reaching critical mass in the wholesale distribution industry. Other trends are just getting started, and this fact makes the ultimate impact on wholesale distribution harder to discern. This report builds on the 2004 report, while extending the analysis and interpretation to reflect our ongoing research during the past 3 years. An overview of the research inputs to this report appears in Appendix A.

Facing the Forces of Change: Lead the Way in the Supply Chain will provide strategic value to your company when it is used as the starting point for more substantive management discussions. Each of the major trends described in this report is designed to pull you away from current events and consider the more complex issue of fundamental change over time.

Consider the growth of private labels, which is a major trend described in Chapter One. Wholesaler-distributors with private labels have deepened their knowledge of their customers' true needs by taking on the role of brand developers and marketers. However, a private label strategy requires the courage to walk away from supplier rebates on selected products in favor of increased margins from customers and buy-side sourcing activities.

The ready availability of global supply sources would lead many wholesale distribution executives to consider private labels. A typical thought process might begin with a look at the relative margin opportunities. Will a private label allow us to get higher product margins? What funds are at risk from the loss of potential supplier rebates or discounts? In the long term, do we risk upsetting our suppliers by moving away from the wholesaler-distributor's traditional role as an extension of a manufacturer's sales and marketing efforts?

Answering these questions will certainly help make the tactical decision, but it will miss the big picture. Do private labels align us more appropriately with customers' needs in our industry? Can we build the brand management capabilities needed for maintaining success over time? Will our shareholders and owners accept higher investments in marketing and product development? How will our corporate culture adjust to an evolution from the sales channel on behalf of manufacturers to a marketer and developer of unique products? How might geopolitics affect future currency rates and our relative cost advantages? These big picture assessments are more qualitative and uncertain and they reflect factors beyond the current year impact on operating profit.

A similar approach can be asked about the demand-driven channels trend described in Chapter Two. In a demand-driven channel, products are pulled down the supply chain to the market based on actual customer demand data. Wholesaler-distributors share point-of-sale and product movement information electronically with their suppliers in this type of channel.

This concept contrasts the more traditional notion of manufacturers pushing products toward the customer through the marketing channel. In this structure, manufacturers only see orders from wholesaler-distributors, and distributors only see orders from their customers. As a result, neither party has visibility into the market consumption or true demand for a product. The lack of timely and accurate information creates turbulence in the supply chain and frequently generates excess inventory at every level.

Moving from the traditional structure to a demand-driven channel requires innovation at every level of the supply chain. Wholesaler-distributors need to send information electronically to suppliers, while simultaneously accepting a new level of visibility and transparency into their operations. Many wholesaler-distributors recoil from the idea of sharing customer information with suppliers, because they fear disintermediation due to direct sales by manufacturers. Others focus only on the additional costs of creating an internal technology infrastructure for gathering and transmitting data.

However, a big picture perspective raises more interesting strategic questions. Which of our suppliers are trustworthy enough to share data? How can we develop an equitable *quid pro quo* for data sharing that will provide new sales or training benefits? What advantages can we gain by helping to shape the standards of data transmittal? How can our internal operations benefit from adopting demand-driven concepts in our own business? Can the demand-driven concept be extended to nontraditional applications, such as data-driven replenishment of customer supplies?

Transparency and accountability will not be uniformly negative if implemented appropriately. Our research found that suppliers plan to measure their channel's performance more closely and make wholesaler-distributors more accountable for both activities and results. Even so, innovative, successful wholesaler-distributors are willing to provide data conveniently to suppliers so that the supply chain can provide customers with the best fulfillment at the lowest costs. The leading wholesale distribution executives welcome a more rigorous approach to channel management by their suppliers, because they recognize the opportunity to further improve their market share and performance.

Chapter Three presents the new sources of profits in the supply chain that can be available to innovative wholesaler-distributors. The new profit models can be best understood in the context of external market developments, such as the growing power of customers documented throughout the long history of the *Facing the Forces of Change*® series.

Wholesale distribution channels were created to carry local inventory, break bulk, aggregate suppliers, provide services, and handle credit for end customers. While these activities remain relevant and necessary, they are no longer uniquely valuable and they can often be obtained from other sources. Customers can push harder for core services at reduced margins from wholesaler-distributors.

Nevertheless, the wholesaler-distributors described in Chapter Three are leading the supply chain by successfully selling fee-based services and redefining their role and function beyond traditional boundaries. The recognition that certain core services have become commoditized has led innovative wholesaler-distributors to position themselves as suppliers of products with related services instead of only reliably providing goods. Their creative actions will ensure a place in the supply chains of tomorrow. The Action Ideas and Questions for Management Discussion in Chapter Three will help wholesale distribution executives determine potential fee-based services that can be offered to suppliers and customers.

Facing the Forces of Change: Lead the Way in the Supply Chain also provides fresh insights about using the Internet to serve customers, a trend described in Chapter Four that is now at a crucial tipping point in wholesale distribution. Internet technology is simultaneously enhancing and challenging the traditional ways that wholesaler-distributors make money. Well-connected, highly informed customers are able to cherry-pick the products and services they need, thereby undermining the basic economic model of a wholesale distribution company. Customers will continue to question the value added by wholesaler-distributors due to the ready availability of information and more sophisticated sourcing techniques as the Internet becomes fully integrated into society.

Innovative wholesaler-distributors are leading in the supply chain by using technology to become more, not less, relevant to their customers. Self-service trends continue to grow as we forecasted 3 years ago in *Facing the Forces of Change: The Road to Opportunity*. As customers become more sophisticated in their use of technology, there are new opportunities for distributors to respond to their customers' expectations by developing innovative online information resources and databases. The growth of online searching will force wholesaler-distributors' Web sites to function as effective sales lead generation tools and will require sales reps to be comfortable selling and communicating using new technologies. In contrast, less-innovative distributors will have an increasingly hard time convincing Internet-savvy customers of their ability to provide support through the entire buying process, from research to service.

The economic environment provides a very favorable context for supply chain leadership by wholesaler-distributors. Nearly all segments of the wholesale distribution industry have experienced extraordinary economic performance in the last few years. Total sales of wholesaler-distributors reached nearly $4 trillion in 2006. Year-to-year quarterly revenue growth averaged a healthy 8.3% from 2003 through mid 2006. Profitability for wholesaler-distributors has also grown during this recent expansion, with operating profits as a percent of sales in 2006 up a full percentage point (1,000 basis points) versus the same period in 2003.[1] (See Exhibit 0-1.)

Nevertheless, the emerging trends in Chapter Five highlight some potential challenges to this favorable environment, such as a slowdown in underlying commodity price inflation that will dampen top-line growth in some lines of trade. The current increase of acquisition activity could fundamentally change industry dynamics. On the other hand, the acquirers may not be able to integrate and operate these companies, and this will lead to a downturn in acquisition activity and the continued success of independent, privately owned wholesaler-distributors.

Wholesaler-distributors are among the biggest beneficiaries of productivity-enhancing technology investments. Productivity growth in the wholesale distribution industry exceeded the overall U.S. business sector by 1.6% in the past 15 years and by 2.5% since 2001. Ongoing productivity will become even more crucial as long-forecasted demographic changes finally begin to affect the wholesale distribution industry. For example, wholesaler-distributors may find themselves competing more aggressively to attract the next generation of junior and middle managers to their companies. They may simultaneously face the retirement of their most knowledgeable and seasoned employees.

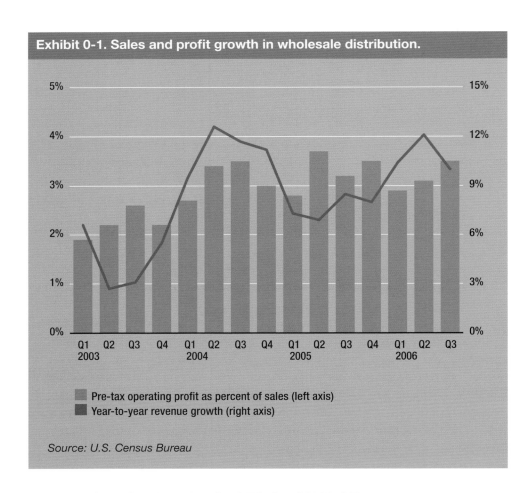

Exhibit 0-1. Sales and profit growth in wholesale distribution.

■ Pre-tax operating profit as percent of sales (left axis)
■ Year-to-year revenue growth (right axis)

Source: U.S. Census Bureau

APPLYING *FACING THE FORCES OF CHANGE* TO YOUR COMPANY

W holesale distribution executives who understand the big picture trends will have the opportunity to lead the way in their lines of trade. Part One allows you to study this big picture before study- ing the details that apply to your markets. It summarizes the four major trends affecting all wholesaler-distributors and presents results for companies of different sizes and that operate in different markets. At the end of each chapter, we also offer Action Ideas with specific strategies and Questions for Management Discussion to help you and your team understand the implications of each trend for your company. In addition to the four major trends, Chapter Five presents three emerging trends whose ultimate importance and impact is highly uncertain.

In addition to the discussion questions provided at the end of Chapters One through Four and possible implications included in Chapter Five, ask yourself the following questions as you study this report.[2]

1. **What is happening in my line of trade today?** We see the trends as likely simply because so many executives told us about their future plans. All the trends in this report are occurring in some part of the wholesale distribution industry. Rather than just relying on your own intuition, ask others in your company to provide their viewpoints. You may also want to provide this report to each member of your senior management and to all of your salespeople so that they can contribute to your strategy discussions.

2. **What does it mean for my customers, suppliers, and competitors?** Try to understand who can benefit or be hurt by these trends. For example, at what point would your suppliers perceive private labels to be a threat to your relationship? What advantages exist for customers if private label products grow or shrink?

3. **What does it mean for my company?** After considering the broader trends, evaluate the specific impact on your own company. It is likely that careful consideration of the trends in this report will suggest new opportunities, investments, and strategies. Many executives may use this report as the basis for an off-site meeting of your company's managers to consider the Questions for Management Discussion in each chapter. They will be better prepared to innovate by putting their day-to-day customer interactions and business responsibilities into a broader perspective of how the industry is changing.

4. **What will have to happen first?** Many trends require some enabling events or activities to fully blossom in an industry. For example, demand-driven channels are based on the exchange of data between suppliers and wholesaler-distributors. Is there a critical mass of wholesaler-distributors that use business management systems to produce the requisite data? Have key suppliers established or adopted standards for data transmission?

5. **What do we do next?** Understand where innovation can benefit your company in the near term and which Action Ideas you can address later. The Action Ideas in Chapters One through Four provide suggested strategic responses to the trends. Naturally, the application of these Action Ideas will depend on your own business situation. The emerging trends summarized in Chapter Five provide possible implications, but the need to act on Action Ideas will depend on the way these trends develop.

To help wholesale distribution executives think through these five questions, Part Two analyzes the results for three major markets in which wholesaler-distributors operate:

- Construction Markets
- Industrial and Commercial Markets
- Retail Consumer Markets.

This approach reflects a combination of end markets, customer types, and products sold. Exhibit 0-2 summarizes this classification approach, while Appendix B relates the NAW member associations to these major markets. Keep in mind that every company is unique. Your company may participate in multiple markets regardless of the products sold. Throughout Part One, we provide helpful cross-references to the detailed findings in Part Two.

Exhibit 0-2. Major markets for wholesaler-distributors.

Major Markets	Representative Products	Representative Customers
CONSTRUCTION MARKETS		
Building Materials	Lumber, Millwork, Floor Covering	Construction Contractors, Builders
Contractor Supplies	Electrical Supplies, Plumbing and Hydronic Heating Equipment and Supplies	Plumbers, Electricians
INDUSTRIAL AND COMMERCIAL MARKETS		
MRO Supplies (Industrial and Commercial)	Medical Supplies, Industrial Paper	Industrial Plants, Multi-Family Housing
OEM and Production Materials	Metals, Electronic Components	Industrial Plants, Contract Manufacturers
RETAIL CONSUMER MARKETS		
Finished Retail Goods	Grocery and Foodservice, Pharmaceuticals	Grocery Stores, Restaurants

Executive Summary

CHAPTER ONE: PRIVATE LABEL PRODUCTS

Private label products—products branded by a wholesaler-distributor—represent a break from the more traditional wholesale distribution approach of reselling manufacturers' branded products. The use of private label strategies by wholesaler-distributors will expand substantially over the next few years. Global sourcing from Asia and South America provides a source of low-cost manufacturing capacity for distributors looking to offer their own private label products.

Private labels will strengthen wholesaler-distributors' relationships with their customers. However, they will strain distributors' relationships with their suppliers by challenging the wholesale distribution channel's traditional role as an extension of a manufacturer's sales and marketing activities. Distributors will need to build new capabilities in manufacturing and design in order to create products with unique, premium benefits. They will also have to select the right opportunities for private labels and manage the new supply chain risks associated with their own products.

CHAPTER TWO: DEMAND-DRIVEN CHANNELS

The term *demand-driven* refers to the idea that products are pulled down the supply chain to the market based on actual customer demand data. It also represents a contrast from the more traditional notion of products in a marketing channel being pushed by manufacturers toward the customer. Both manufacturers and distributors will be able to manage their respective inventories better when demand-based information is shared. Three key enabling factors for a demand-driven channel will become more prominent over the next 5 years, thereby creating the conditions for demand-driven channels in many wholesale distribution lines of trade. These factors are

- An automated order stream from wholesaler-distributors
- Upstream visibility into actual demand from the customers of wholesaler-distributors
- Adoption of automatic product identification technologies by wholesaler-distributors.

Wholesaler-distributors can succeed with demand-driven channels by developing appropriate supply chain data transmission standards in their lines of trade, evaluating new profit streams from data transmissions to suppliers, and applying demand-driven concepts to their own businesses.

CHAPTER THREE: NEW PROFIT MODELS

Manufacturers will increase their share of a wholesaler-distributor's profit margin from product distribution, and this will lead to greater use of pay-for-performance channel compensation models by manufacturers. Wholesaler-distributors will need to understand whether their companies are truly profitable channel partners.

Nevertheless, wholesaler-distributors can benefit from better measurement of performance and can derive new profit streams in the supply chain. One example is outsourced fulfillment as a fee-based service to traditional suppliers. This allows distributors to beat back the threat from logistics companies. Many wholesaler-distributors are also successfully creating new profit models through fee-based services to customers, and this trend will keep growing across most wholesale distribution industry segments.

Ongoing success will require wholesaler-distributors to master the financial dynamics of a services business, which are different from a product distribution business. Wholesaler-distributors will also need to monitor new developments at competing logistics companies and avoid their overconfidence in the unique value of their own logistics prowess.

CHAPTER FOUR: CONNECTED CUSTOMERS

Wholesaler-distributors must fully embrace the Internet in their business activities now that it is a normal part of everyday life in the United States and Canada. Online search capability is becoming a primary way for customers to find new suppliers, so wholesaler-distributors should shift their marketing resources online to reach potential customers who are looking for suppliers. Online collaboration tools, such as online work spaces and virtual trade shows, will emerge as new ways for wholesaler-distributors to interact with their customers. However, customers will increasingly gather information from other customers, thereby bypassing traditional marketing messages from both upstream manufacturers and their wholesaler-distributors.

Adoption of self-service technologies, which has grown significantly in the past 3 years, will continue, so wholesaler-distributors must allow customers to gain information, place an order, and solve simple problems themselves when appropriate. Success in the ever-evolving online business environment will require wholesaler-distributors to use their Web sites as an effective sales lead generation tool and information resource to respond to their customers and to teach their sales reps to sell and communicate using new technologies.

CHAPTER FIVE: EMERGING TRENDS

The wholesale distribution industry is going through a very active wave of merger and acquisition activity that is led by both strategic buyers and financial buyers, such as private equity firms. Although executives in most markets expect continued acquisition activity, there is little consensus about the ultimate impact on the wholesale distribution industry.

The U.S. workforce is becoming older and more diverse as the baby boom generation ages, mirroring broader changes in the U.S. population. These demographic changes could have substantial impacts on the wholesale distribution industry, although there will not be a single point in time when these demographic changes trigger a particular crisis in the wholesale distribution industry. Distributors may face the retirement of their most knowledgeable and seasoned employees, while simultaneously competing more aggressively to attract the next generation of junior and middle managers to their companies.

Wholesale distribution executives must also recognize that unusually high commodity price inflation has made revenue growth much easier to achieve. Wholesaler-distributors are going to have to work harder for real growth as the commodity cycle changes, and this will require a more strategic and focused approach. Wholesaler-distributors will benefit by using demand-driven models (Chapter Two) and evaluating new profit sources (Chapter Three).

CHAPTER SIX: CONSTRUCTION MARKETS

Wholesaler-distributors of building materials and contractor supplies have shown consistent growth during the past 5 years due to strong residential construction activity, the rebound in commercial construction, and the growth of remodeling and repair work. The combination of many small customers and multiple specialties supports a diverse set of wholesale distribution lines of trade that are typically organized around product type.

The private label products trend will affect wholesaler-distributors of building materials much more than contractor supplies wholesaler-distributors. In contrast, the demand-driven channels trend will have a smaller impact on building materials markets than on any other market covered in this report. The impact on contractor supplies markets will be greater due in part to the connection to maintenance, repair, and operations (MRO) markets. The consolidation of builders is changing wholesaler-distributors' profit sources and this creates new opportunities for both fee-based services to customers and fee-for-service logistics to suppliers. The fragmented nature of contractor supplies markets suggests relatively fast penetration for the connected customers trend.

CHAPTER SEVEN: INDUSTRIAL AND COMMERCIAL MARKETS

Domestic manufacturing continues to undergo a dramatic transformation, which challenges industrial MRO and original equipment manufacturer (OEM) wholesaler-distributors. Manufacturing employment has not rebounded following the unprecedented decline that began in 2000. In contrast, the commercial MRO business is much less cyclical than the industrial business because it is tied to many diverse segments of the U.S. economy.

The private label products trend is well established in both MRO and OEM markets. Almost one-half of MRO supplies distributors and nearly two-thirds of OEM and production materials distributors currently offer private label products. Demand-driven channels are coming to industrial and commercial wholesale distribution markets. By 2012, many MRO supplies wholesaler-distributors and OEM and production materials wholesaler-distributors expect to share point-of-sale data with suppliers.

Wholesale distribution executives in industrial and commercial markets expect important shifts in the composition of their gross margin. The shift to manufacturer-led compensation is most pronounced in OEM and production materials markets, whereas MRO supplies distributors are benefiting from fee-for-service offerings to customers. The Internet will grow to be a crucial sourcing tool in these markets, although the growth rates in Web site ordering have slowed in the past few years.

CHAPTER EIGHT: RETAIL CONSUMER MARKETS

Retail sectors are becoming more concentrated and increasingly dominated by a handful of large, multiple-location chain stores, warehouse clubs, home centers, and supercenters. Wholesaler-distributors serving retail markets face a shrinking number of potential customers even though overall retail sales continue to expand. As a result, more than one-half of wholesaler-distributors in retail markets offer their private label products, which often provide unique items to help their small retail customers compete against the retail giants.

Wholesaler-distributors in retail markets share data with more suppliers than in other markets, and this reflects the fact that the demand-driven concept originated in retail industries. Similar to other markets, wholesaler-distributors in retail markets expect that manufacturers will take on more responsibility for a distributor's profit margin from product distribution. However, fee-for-service payments from customers will be harder to get than in other markets. Online ordering will see substantial growth, while ordering methods that are still termed *traditional* in other customer segments will see a sustained decline.

Part One

Trends Changing Wholesale Distribution

Chapters One through Four summarize these four major trends affecting all wholesaler-distributors:

One Private Label Products
Two Demand-Driven Channels
Three New Profit Models
Four Connected Customers.

Certain trends will not equally affect distributors of all sizes or that serve different customer types. Part One also presents selected findings by revenue size and customer type, along with cross-references to the market detail in Part Two.

Chapters One through Four contain the following sections:
- **Summary** highlighting the most important conclusions
- **Data Points** summarizing specific quantitative findings
- A detailed discussion of the study's findings
- **Action Ideas** with specific strategy concepts for your company
- **Questions for Management Discussion** to help you and your management team understand the implications of the trend for your company.

Chapter Five reviews three emerging trends whose ultimate importance and impact is highly uncertain.

CHAPTER ONE

Private Label Products

SUMMARY

Private label products—those products branded by a wholesaler-distributor—represent a break from the more traditional wholesale distribution approach of reselling manufacturers' branded products. The use of private label strategies by wholesaler-distributors will expand substantially over the next few years. Global sourcing from Asia and South America provides a source of low-cost manufacturing capacity for wholesaler-distributors that are looking to offer their own private label products.

Private labels will strengthen wholesaler-distributors' relationships with their customers. However, they will strain distributors' relationships with their suppliers by challenging the wholesale distribution channel's traditional role as an extension of a manufacturer's sales and marketing activities. Wholesaler-distributors will need to build new capabilities in manufacturing and design in order to create products with unique, premium benefits. They will also have to select the right opportunities for private labels and manage the new supply chain risks associated with sourcing these products.

Data Points
- About 43% of wholesaler-distributors currently market their own private label products.
- Total merchandise imports into the United States were $1.7 trillion in 2005. China's share of imports is now 15% and that is up from 8% in 2000.
- About 24% of wholesaler-distributors sell to customers who centralize purchasing authority for multiple locations within the customer's organization.

MANY WHOLESALER-DISTRIBUTORS WILL MARKET THEIR PRIVATE LABEL PRODUCTS

We use the term *private label* to include both products manufactured by a wholesaler-distributor under contract, as well as more traditional branded products that are owned or acquired by a wholesale distribution company. A private label product's brand may incorporate the wholesaler-distributor's company name or it may use a distinct name. In both cases, marketing of these brands contrasts with a more traditional approach of reselling manufacturers' branded products.

As predicted in the 2004 *Facing the Forces of Change: The Road to Opportunity* report, the use of private label strategies by wholesaler-distributors will expand substantially over the next few years. (See Exhibit 1-1.)

Private label products offer these benefits to wholesaler-distributors:

- **Buy-side margin.** Private label products can be priced lower than comparable national brand products, especially when sourced directly from an overseas manufacturer. Since private label products are less expensive to purchase, a distributor can earn a higher margin, even when the products are priced at a discount to national brand products.

- **Sell-side profitability.** A wholesaler-distributor's private label products offer the opportunity for increased profitability by capturing the *branded* margin that would otherwise flow to an upstream manufacturer. The distributor also gains the ability to control the entire profit stream from production to sale, allowing for more flexible sales compensation models and higher commissions to drive sales. For example, a distributor can reduce the advertising overhead of a national brand manufacturer, especially on certain products for which customers see no value differentiation. Capturing the branded margin will generally incur higher costs for brand management, which we will discuss later in the Action Ideas section of this chapter.

- **Differentiated product assortment.** A private label brand name can be exclusive to a wholesaler-distributor and provide a point of differentiation. For example, some wholesaler-distributors find that they can fill gaps in the marketplace by offering the *good* (value) alternative in a *good/better/best* hierarchy. Availability can be another point of differentiation. A private label product can be sourced from multiple manufacturing companies and this gives a distributor the opportunity for more consistent product availability than when sourcing from uniquely branded manufacturers.

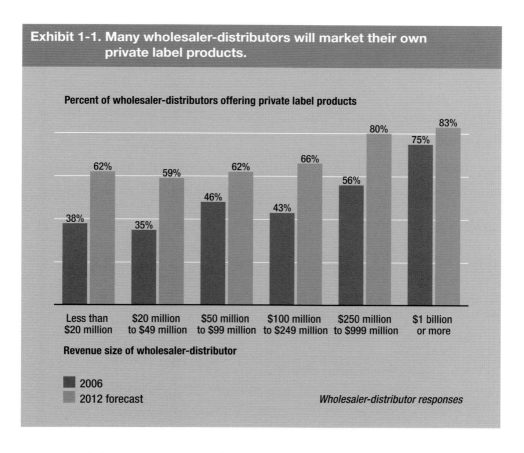

Exhibit 1-1. Many wholesaler-distributors will market their own private label products.

Percent of wholesaler-distributors offering private label products

Revenue size	2006	2012 forecast
Less than $20 million	38%	62%
$20 million to $49 million	35%	59%
$50 million to $99 million	46%	62%
$100 million to $249 million	43%	66%
$250 million to $999 million	56%	80%
$1 billion or more	75%	83%

Revenue size of wholesaler-distributor

■ 2006
■ 2012 forecast

Wholesaler-distributor responses

Private label products first gained prominence in consumer goods retailing. According to the Private Label Manufacturers Association (www.plma.com), private label brands now account for one of every five items sold in U.S. supermarkets, drug chains, and mass merchandisers. Retail private label consumer grocery products, which have a 16% share of U.S. sales, are priced on average 28% lower than national brand competitors.[3] However, retail private label products have gross margins averaging 15% to 20% higher than those of national brand products. In some cases, consumer retailers have introduced *premium* private label brands that compete effectively at the high end with manufacturers' branded products.

Many wholesaler-distributors already offer highly sophisticated private label programs. **Interline Brands** (www.interlinebrands.com), a direct marketer and distributor of MRO products, receives 25% of its sales from private label brands, such as Premier faucets, Centurion air conditioners, Lumina light bulbs, and ProPlus retail plumbing accessories.

To support its brands, Interline operates a consumer-oriented product marketing Web site for the Premier Faucet Collection (www.premierfaucet.com). This Web site features images and technical information so that Interline's plumbing contractor customers can showcase the products to household consumers. The Web site also allows Interline to provide new project leads to its contractor customers because the "where to buy" section states: "Premier Faucets are sold exclusively to trade professionals. Please complete the following form and you will be contacted by a Premier representative."

The evolution of **Thermo Fisher Scientific** (www.fisherscientific.com) illustrates the profit impact of private label products. The company, whose roots in product distribution go back to 1902, dramatically increased its private label product mix with the acquisition of two branded manufacturing companies in 2002. In 2006, about two-thirds of the company's revenue was generated from the sales of higher-margin proprietary products. Operating profit as a percentage of revenues had almost doubled to 13.2% because the company gained the branded manufacturing margin in its mix.

GLOBAL SOURCING IS ACCELERATING PRIVATE LABEL GROWTH

Countries in Asia and South America currently provide a source of low-cost manufacturing capacity for companies looking to offer their own private label products. On average, 43% of wholesaler-distributors currently market their own private label products. About 57% of these companies source their private label products from an overseas plant. By 2012, 81% of these wholesaler-distributors expect to be sourcing overseas. (See Exhibit 1-2.)

The lower costs and ready availability of overseas sourcing opportunities accelerate the ability of wholesaler-distributors to get their own value-priced private label products manufactured. A related alternative is to locate quality goods without a U.S. presence or brand name and then brand the products for the U.S. market. As we discuss in the Action Ideas section, external factors could alter these favorable economics or create undesirable risks.

Our interviews and surveys revealed that wholesaler-distributors are importing private labels from a wide range of countries, including China, Korea, Taiwan, India, (South) Chile, Canada, and Mexico. However, we heard most about China, which has emerged as an important source of imported products throughout the U.S. economy. Consider the following facts about China sourcing:

- China's unit labor costs are much lower than developed countries in North America and Europe even when those costs are adjusted for lower average worker productivity. Given a rural population that is three times as large as the entire U.S. population, many experts expect China's low-cost labor advantage to be sustainable for at least a generation.

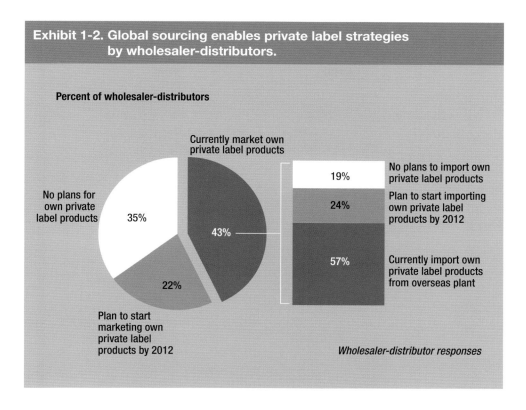

Exhibit 1-2. Global sourcing enables private label strategies by wholesaler-distributors.

Percent of wholesaler-distributors

Currently market own private label products

No plans for own private label products — 35%

43%

22%

Plan to start marketing own private label products by 2012

No plans to import own private label products — 19%

Plan to start importing own private label products by 2012 — 24%

Currently import own private label products from overseas plant — 57%

Wholesaler-distributor responses

- China's manufactured exports to the world are now estimated to exceed those of the United States, whereas U.S.-manufactured exports were more than double those of China in 2001.[4] Total merchandise imports into the United States reached $1.7 trillion in 2005, and that is up 37% from 2000. During that same period, imports from China grew from 8% of total U.S. merchandise imports to 15%.

- Consumer electronics and industrial goods are quickly replacing low-tech products such as apparel. In 2005, $53.1 billion of electronics and electrical products were imported from China, and this represents just over one-quarter of the total U.S. imports of these product categories. (See Exhibit 1-3.)

- Imports from China represent primarily contract manufacturing relationships by non-Chinese companies. In 2005, only 26% of imports from mainland China were between related parties, compared to almost 80% of imports from Japan. *Related party trade* includes trade by U.S. companies with their subsidiaries abroad, as well as trade by U.S. subsidiaries of foreign companies with their parent companies.

Exhibit 1-3. U.S. merchandise imports from China.

Product	Total Imports from China (billions)	China as Percent of Total U.S. Imports
Electric Machinery, Stereo and TV Equipment and Parts	$53.1	26%
Nuclear Reactors, Boilers, Machinery, etc.; Parts	$52.7	24%
Apparel and Footwear	$29.5	33%
Toys, Games, and Sports Equipment; Parts and Accessories	$19.1	78%
Furniture and Bedding	$17.1	46%
Plastics	$6.6	21%
Leather Products	$6.3	72%
Iron or Steel Articles	$6.2	26%
Vehicles and Parts (except Rail and Tramways)	$4.2	2%
Optical, Photographic, Medical, Surgical Equipment	$4.1	9%
All Other Products	$44.5	6%
Total	**$243.5**	**15%**

Source: Pembroke Consulting analyses of U.S. Department of Commerce data

- Wal-Mart is the largest single company sourcing products in China and it sourced an estimated $22 billion of products in 2005.[5] This figure includes products purchased directly from China, as well as products made in China for another company and then sold to Wal-Mart. For comparison, Wal-Mart sourced an estimated $2 billion of products from China in 1998.

In our interviews, most wholesale distribution executives expect some or all of these countries to continue providing favorable sourcing opportunities over the next few years. However, this environment is not guaranteed to continue forever. In the Action Ideas section of this chapter, we highlight risk factors that could increase the total landed cost of global sourcing.

For example, **Do it Best Corp**. (www.doitbestcorp.com), a U.S.-based, member-owned distributor of lumber, hardware, and building materials with annual revenues of more than $3 billion, opened Asian offices in Hong Kong and Hangzhou in 2006. At the present time, the company sources products globally in all product categories, including private label products under the Do it Best®, Do it®, Home Impressions™, and SteelPro™ brand names. Although the company has sourced from China since the mid 1990s, the new operation in Hangzhou puts company management physically closer to manufacturing, packaging, design, and inspection.

W.W. Grainger, Inc. (www.grainger.com), a distributor of facilities maintenance products, is also moving aggressively into global sourcing of private label products. The company sourced more than 9,000 SKUs equaling $400 million in sales. These products, which came primarily from China and Taiwan, had gross margins that are about 20% higher than other products sold through the company's branch network.

PRIVATE LABEL PRODUCTS WILL STRENGTHEN DISTRIBUTORS' RELATIONSHIPS WITH CUSTOMERS

A distributor's value-priced private label product offers a less expensive alternative to a branded product. This option simultaneously grows margins for the distributor and aligns the distributor more closely with its customer's objectives. An executive at a materials handling equipment distributor said: "We all will have to source the most valued and competitive products available to our customer base. The world's ability to share and develop technology in manufacturing is flattening."

Strategic sourcing programs create opportunities for a wholesaler-distributor to grow private label brands by providing a new source of savings for large, multiple-location customers. Understanding the role of sourcing compliance can provide a wholesaler-distributor with new opportunities to grow its private label products.

Chapter Two in the 2004 report described the growth of *strategic sourcing*, a structured process by which larger, multiple-location customers attempt to leverage their purchasing power. The strategic sourcing process encourages customers to become more confrontational; they rely increasingly more on sophisticated sourcing initiatives and they maximize their volume-buying discounts by standardizing the products and brands they purchase.

Strategic sourcing consists of three major activities:

1. **Assessment and spend analysis.** The first step involves aggregating and analyzing internal purchasing data to measure spending by distributor, product, application, and location. The customer develops a complete view of total spending activity by identifying the product baskets with the greatest potential savings.

2. **Sourcing and contracting.** At this stage, customers attempt to leverage buying power across work sites and within product categories using tools such as national contracts, vendor reduction, and reverse auctions.

3. **Implementation.** To achieve the benefits of sourcing, customers attempt to enforce buying discipline by individual buyers within their organizations. Centralized purchasing departments attempt to clamp down on individual buyers who buy from nonspecified distributors, buy the wrong products, or pay higher prices than they should.

Strategic sourcing will continue to grow. Our 2006 survey showed the expected growth in two ways that customers will control *how* and *where* individual buyers buy products. (See Exhibit 1-4.)

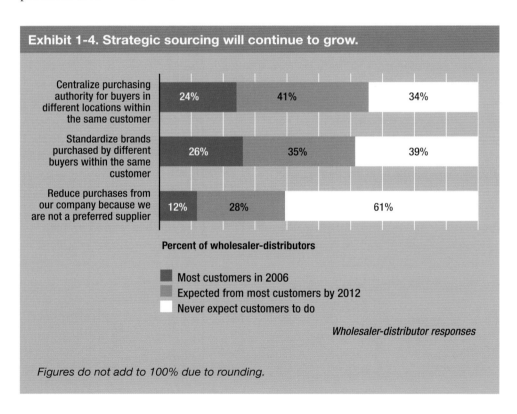

Exhibit 1-4. Strategic sourcing will continue to grow.

Centralized Purchasing

About 24% of wholesaler-distributors sell to customers that centralize purchasing authority for multiple locations within the customer's organization. Another 41% expect this trend to affect most of their customers within 5 years. Wholesaler-distributors that sell to industrial buyers will experience this trend most sharply. In contrast, distributors that sell to contractors expect almost 40% of their customers to never attempt this strategy.

Brand Standardization

About 26% of wholesaler-distributors expect customers to standardize brands purchased by different buyers within the same organization. A further 35% expect that most of their customers will employ this tactic in the future, and this is similar to the results for more centralized purchasing.

As a result, spending analyses suggest untapped volume purchasing along with opportunities to substitute wholesaler-distributors' private label products for national brands. As the power of the purchasing department grows, individual buyers within a customer's organization lose the ability to purchase personally preferred brands. The customer realizes the direct, hard-dollar cost savings from substitution of private label brands.

Private label products also deliver value to smaller customers that do little formal strategic sourcing, especially for products seen as commodity items by customers. A wholesaler-distributor has an opportunity to offer an alternative to price-sensitive customers without sacrificing quality. One wholesale distribution executive explained the benefit to his smaller customers as follows: "Large manufacturers have relabeled generic accessory products for many years, thus capturing extraordinary gross margins from accessory sales. We sell what are, in essence, the exact same things more economically."

PRIVATE LABEL GROWTH WILL STRAIN DISTRIBUTORS' RELATIONSHIPS WITH SUPPLIERS

Private labels are a challenge to the wholesale distribution channel's traditional role as an extension of a manufacturer's sales and marketing activities. Private label brands change the balance of power in channel relationships. Power is the ability of one channel member to get another channel member to do what it otherwise would not have done. In practice, power is obtained when one channel member (the manufacturer or the distributor) controls resources that are valued by the other company.

Access to customers is a critical resource influenced by the wholesale distribution channel. The power of the wholesale distribution channel increases when the customer relies on the distributor to provide a value-priced private label product. Customer-initiated strategic sourcing agreements limit the influence of brand-level marketing on product purchasing decisions.

Vendor consolidation becomes a means by which distributors can meet customer demands for brand consolidation and strategic sourcing savings. Rather than stocking a proliferation of comparable products, wholesaler-distributors are likely to reduce the number of brands and SKUs carried in categories with private labels. This simultaneously increases a distributor's bargaining power with manufacturers and makes its internal operations more efficient.

Now that we've looked closely at the private label products trend, let's look at specific strategies within the following Action Ideas to help you better understand the implications of this trend for your company. This chapter closes with Questions for Management Discussion that you and your team can tackle right away.

ACTION IDEAS

1. Identify the right opportunities for private labels.

Certain product lines or categories have greater potential for a wholesaler-distributor's private label product. Exhibit 1-5 provides a series of questions designed to assess brand value.[6] These questions can be answered from the perspective of a single product line or an entire product category.

These questions provide insights into situations in which a proliferation of comparable products has created many brands that add little value to customers. Private label potential is greatest for product lines or categories with more "No" answers.

Here are representative verbatim comments from wholesale distribution executives describing the factors that made private label brands successful for their companies, along with their companies' primary product lines:

- "Customers demand value for their money and are not brand loyal on everyday items. The products must work well to compete. When you have both elements, customers will tend to try and buy more of the private brand." (printing paper)

- "Our vendors would not differentiate the product, packaging, or order number to assist us in competing. We provide a label to our small retail customers that cannot be found in other retail outlets." (security hardware)

Exhibit 1-5. Assessing private label potential.

Private label potential is greatest for product lines or categories with more "No" answers.

1. Do customers perceive each of the branded products in the category to be truly unique?	Yes	No
2. Are there fewer than three direct competitors?	Yes	No
3. Are customers for these products highly price sensitive?	Yes	No
4. Do suppliers of branded products have a larger installed base of users?	Yes	No
5. Is each branded product's quality measurably better than competitors in the opinions of customers?	Yes	No
6. Do customers insist on the branded products when ordering?	Yes	No

---

- "We have the most success selling commodity items that the customer perceives have no value." (landscape irrigation supplies)

- "In general, chemicals and fasteners have been our most successful private label products. Products that provide superior performance and are not marketed by national brands (electric terminals, welding) are also successful." (MRO products)

2. Provide unique benefits with private label products.

Success will require distributors to act more like marketers. Manufacturers have brand managers who make product and promotion decisions for their brands. Similarly, wholesaler-distributors will have to position their private label products as more than simply lower-cost versions of competing products if they want to earn higher profits.

Consider **Arbill Safety Products** (www.arbill.com), a third-generation distributor that provides safety products and services to customers in a wide range of industries. In addition to stocking more than 4,000 products from all major branded manufacturers, Arbill has offered its own private label products for more than 20 years. The products are manufactured under contract in eight countries throughout Asia and are received in container quantities into the Philadelphia port close to Arbill's main warehouse.

As part of the company's growth to serve larger, national customers, Arbill began branding its private label product line under the TRULINE® brand. Arbill can differentiate the brand in the marketplace by controlling the entire value chain from design to delivery.

The brand, which is used for a wide set of personal protection product lines, has a unique logo and high-quality packaging. Customers can request specific features to existing TRULINE® products; this allows Arbill to produce a customized, unique product for customers with special requirements. To meet customer demand, Arbill offers a better quality product in selected product lines than the manufacturer-branded products on the market.

Arbill's direct relationships with overseas factories allow the company to provide these benefits from the TRULINE® brand at a competitive price versus comparable manufacturer brands. However, certain products can be priced higher when they provide higher quality or additional value to the customer.

3. Understand the supply chain responsibilities of private label products.

Wholesale distribution executives who plan private label products must recognize the additional responsibilities facing the managers in their companies. New activities could include product design, factory selection, testing, packaging, and importing. Some aspects such as customs brokerage can be outsourced to a partner, while others may need to be controlled in house. For example, Arbill Safety Products cannot develop products with unique benefits unless the company leverages its internal customer knowledge and relationships.

There are also legal risks. For example, a purchase order with a major branded manufacturer often indemnifies a wholesaler-distributor against certain product liability risks. In contrast, a wholesaler-distributor takes on that risk when sourcing and selling its own product.

Some risks are also tied to global sourcing. Although sourcing from China or other countries offers lower product costs, supply chain expenses and risks can reduce or eliminate any potential savings. Examples of expenses and risks include:

- **Longer lead times**. Geographic distance makes planning more difficult because lead times are much longer and more uncertain, thereby inflating inventories in the supply chain. Ironically, global sourcing strategies by wholesaler-distributors represent a trend opposed to the demand-driven channels trend described in Chapter Two.

- **Lack of visibility.** International supply chains are less automated, so some of the technologies and processes described in Chapters Two and Four will not be available. Internet-based technology is enabling a new level of visibility for monitoring the progress of transactions. One best practices study of international logistics identified Internet-based automation as a key success factor for global sourcing.[7] This study found that a majority of companies were not tracking activities throughout the global sourcing process.

- **Unanticipated logistics costs.** Global sourcing increases direct shipping and transportation costs. However, most companies without international experience lack internal benchmarks for understanding freight costs and managing discrepancies. In addition, China's logistics and transportation infrastructure is much less developed and highly fragmented. There are several hundred thousand logistics companies in China compared to fewer than 10,000 in the United States. Some research companies estimate that trucking a 40-foot container from Beijing to Shanghai can cost as much as $400 in tolls (along toll roads). The alternative is nontoll roads and endless congestion.[8]

- **Currency risks.** China's growth as a source of low-cost U.S. imports was partly due to China's central bank policy pegging the yuan at 12 cents to the dollar from 1994 to 2005. In July 2005, China revalued the yuan by 2.1% and began referencing its value against a basket of currencies. China is also embarking on a policy of tightening monetary policy to head off inflationary pressures created by the country's rapid growth.

QUESTIONS FOR MANAGEMENT DISCUSSION

Here are discussion questions for your management team. Please review the detailed results for your specific customers and markets in Chapters Six through Eight before discussing these topics.

1. What are the most successful private label brands offered to customers by wholesaler-distributors (our company or a competitor) in our line of trade? Why have these products been so successful? What lessons can we learn about developing future private label brands for our customers?

2. What new opportunities for our private label brands can be created as part of a customer's strategic sourcing program? Which of our customers would benefit from brand standardization and rationalization across locations or buyers within their organizations?

3. Will our private label products remain competitive if the price/cost advantage begins to shrink? Which product lines could be developed or improved to provide unique product benefits to customers beyond price? How can we improve our marketing or product features to achieve premium positioning for some of our private label products?

4. How have our suppliers reacted to the growth of private label brands by wholesaler-distributors? What strategies are they likely to use with their wholesale distribution channel as private labels continue to grow? How can we benefit from our suppliers' likely reactions?

5. In which product lines, if any, should we avoid creating private label brands? Where do we want to avoid competing with our suppliers?

CHAPTER TWO

Demand-Driven Channels

SUMMARY

The term *demand-driven* refers to the idea that products are pulled down the supply chain to the market based on actual customer demand data. It also represents a contrast from the more traditional notion of products in a marketing channel being pushed by manufacturers toward customers. Both manufacturers and distributors will be able to manage their respective inventories better when demand-based information is shared. Wholesaler-distributors can succeed with demand-driven channels by developing appropriate supply chain data transmission standards in their lines of trade, evaluating new profit streams from data transmissions to suppliers, and applying demand-driven concepts to their own businesses.

Data Points
- Larger manufacturers electronically receive 46% of sales from their channel and expect to receive 70% by 2012.
- The average wholesaler-distributor stocks 340 suppliers in inventory.
- In 2006, at least 60% of wholesaler-distributors shared at least some point-of-sale data with their suppliers.

DEMAND-DRIVEN CHANNELS COME
TO WHOLESALE DISTRIBUTION CHANNELS

Our research found that the demand-driven supply chain philosophy is beginning to take root in the business-to-business supply chains in which wholesaler-distributors play a major role.

In a demand-driven channel, shipments should respond to real-time or near real-time (daily) information that is shared across a network of customers, wholesaler-distributors, and suppliers. Wholesaler-distributors share point-of-sale and product movement information electronically with their suppliers.

In a more traditional structure where manufacturers only see orders from wholesaler-distributors, and the distributors, in turn, only see orders from their customers, neither party has visibility into the market consumption (true demand) for a product. As we discuss later in this chapter, manufacturers may have many legitimate business reasons for maintaining this system.

The amplification and information distortion that ripples up the supply chain when demand data are not shared is often referred to as the *bullwhip effect*.[9] The bullwhip analogy comes from the fact that a small change ripples forward to create large variations, just like flicking your wrist causes the end of a whip to jump.

The uncertainty and variability caused by a lack of true demand information leads every participant in the supply chain to stockpile extra inventory. It is caused by a combination of poor or inaccurate forecasts, promotional purchases by the channel, and other failures to provide true visibility to upstream suppliers. Consider the following two representative situations that could create this supply chain effect:

- **Perceived demand.** Customers perceive that demand is unexpectedly increasing. In response, customers begin increasing order size with their wholesaler-distributors to build safety stock. As a result, wholesaler-distributors increase order sizes with their suppliers, who then begin increasing production and building inventory in response to new channel orders. If the sales increase does not materialize, suppliers and wholesaler-distributors are stuck with excess inventory.

- **Forward buying.** The market share goals of manufacturers can contribute to excessive promotional activity in order to stimulate sales. Wholesaler-distributors place larger orders to take advantage of volume price discounts, short-term manufacturer promotions, or forward-buying opportunities. Such business decisions, which can be sensible and profit-enhancing for an individual wholesaler-distributor, create orders from the wholesale distribution channel that do not reflect the true pattern of sales to customers. We discuss the impact of manufacturer market share goals later in this chapter.

In both situations, the variability in wholesaler-distributors' orders to suppliers becomes much greater than the variability in actual usage by customers, and this creates the bullwhip effect to ripple up a wholesale distribution channel. These problems can become acute for wholesaler-distributors that operate in highly complex distribution channels with many intermediaries, because sales data can become more highly distorted.

Both manufacturers and distributors will be able to manage their respective inventories better when demand-based information is shared. Manufacturers can improve production planning and achieve more stable production runs with more consistent ordering patterns from distributors. Many manufacturers use the information to help them forecast production, plan new product launches, or measure share on a market-by-market basis. Wholesaler-distributors that share information with suppliers should expect higher service levels from those suppliers. Wholesaler-distributors that gather better data from customers, such as through vendor managed inventory (VMI) arrangements, can simultaneously reduce inventory levels and the risk of stock outs.

Demand-driven channels are also valuable when supply is limited due to production problems or unexpectedly strong customer demand. In a demand-driven channel, scarce products can be allocated based on actual demand patterns rather than on historic distributor sales patterns. A wholesaler-distributor will lose the incentive to place extra orders within a manufacturer's product allocation system, so fewer customers or other distributors are disadvantaged. Since the manufacturer receives forecasts based on true demand instead of on channel orders, it can ramp up production appropriately.

There are three key enabling factors for a demand-driven channel:

- An automated order stream from wholesaler-distributors
- Upstream visibility into actual demand from the customers of distributors
- Adoption of automatic product identification technologies by distributors.

All of these factors will become more prominent over the next 5 years, and this will create the conditions for demand-driven channels in many wholesale distribution lines of trade.

THE WHOLESALE DISTRIBUTION ORDER STREAM
WILL BE AUTOMATED

One foundational element of a demand-driven channel is the real-time analysis of orders from the wholesale distribution channel, which only occurs with automation of the inbound order stream from distributors. In this context, automation requires orders to be submitted in an electronic format that can be automatically read into a supplier's system, such as Electronic Data Interchange (EDI), or placed on a supplier's Web site. Orders submitted via e-mail by a wholesaler-distributor are not considered part of an automated order stream because e-mails must be rekeyed rather than imported automatically.

Our survey of manufacturers (suppliers to wholesaler-distributors) shows that electronic order submission from the wholesale distribution channel is increasing rapidly. (See Exhibit 2-1.) The findings include:

- In 2006, small manufacturers received 11% of sales volume via automated electronic orders from the wholesale distribution channel. This is almost twice the volume received by smaller manufacturers reported for 2003 in *Facing the Forces of Change: The Road to Opportunity*. Manufacturers expect this volume to nearly triple by 2012.

- About 26% of midsized manufacturers' order stream is currently automated. This figure is expected to more than double to 55% by 2012.

- Larger manufacturers electronically received 46% of sales from their wholesale distribution channel in 2006. Channel order automation is forecast to continue with larger manufacturers expecting to receive 70% of sales via electronic order submission from the wholesale distribution channel.

These forecasts primarily reflect the growing use of EDI for automating order stream from the wholesale distribution channel. As predicted in the 2004 report, EDI remains a viable technology standard that can still perform at acceptable levels and costs. The benefits of using the 25-year-old EDI standards are well documented, such as reduced labor costs for ordering and lower error rates. EDI transactions continue migrating to the Internet and away from proprietary one-to-one systems.

Exhibit 2-1. Suppliers expect a sharp increase in electronic orders from their wholesaler-distributors.

Wholesaler-Distributor Ordering Methods by Revenue Size of Manufacturer	Percent of Sales Received via Automated Electronic Orders from Wholesaler-Distributors	
	2006	2012 Forecast
LESS THAN $50 MILLION		
Via supplier Web site	1%	12%
Via third-party Web site	1%	1%
Via Electronic Data Interchange (EDI)	9%	19%
Electronic Total	**11%**	**32%**
$50 MILLION TO $500 MILLION		
Via supplier Web site	6%	21%
Via third-party Web site	1%	2%
Via Electronic Data Interchange (EDI)	19%	32%
Electronic Total	**26%**	**55%**
$500 MILLION OR MORE		
Via supplier Web site	7%	20%
Via third-party Web site	1%	2%
Via Electronic Data Interchange (EDI)	38%	48%
Electronic Total	**46%**	**70%**

Responses from manufacturers (suppliers to wholesaler-distributors)

Note that EDI order submission is expected to remain a more important source of electronic orders from wholesaler-distributors than orders placed on a manufacturer-supplier's own Web site. This is a contrast to the dynamic facing wholesaler-distributors. The average wholesaler-distributor stocks 340 suppliers in inventory. Even though purchasing is usually concentrated with less than 30 suppliers, purchasing agents at a wholesaler-distributor would consider it unreasonably burdensome to visit more than 300 different Web sites to place orders.

SUPPLIERS WILL GAIN VISIBILITY INTO WHOLESALER-DISTRIBUTORS' PRODUCT MOVEMENT DATA

Another key aspect of demand-driven channels involves allowing upstream suppliers to access sales and product movement as close to the end customer as possible. For example, a manufacturer's forecasts, inventory purchases, and other channel planning decisions can be based on changes in actual customer sales activity by wholesaler-distributors rather than on using internal forecasts or orders from distribution channel members. In practice, visibility translates into having the downstream channel member (a wholesaler-distributor or retailer) share point-of-sale data.

Although many wholesaler-distributors feel uncomfortable with data sharing, information transparency among trading partners is common practice in retail distribution channels. Consider **Wal-Mart's** Retail Link® (www.walmart.com), a custom-built Web site that suppliers are required to use for VMI. Wal-Mart provides real-time access to a supplier's actual sales data by store. Suppliers can also review inventory levels, returns, and adjustments. All suppliers must utilize these data to maintain very high service levels to Wal-Mart.

While this system clearly benefits Wal-Mart, its suppliers also benefit from more timely and accurate insights into end customer sales. For example, manufacturers supplying Wal-Mart can improve production planning and achieve more stable production runs with more predictable ordering patterns from distributors. Many manufacturers will want to go further and gain information to help them forecast, plan new product launches, and measure share on a market-by-market basis. Research studies consistently find that upstream suppliers that use demand management techniques have fewer days of sales in inventory and higher inventory turns.

Similar data-sharing practices will impact wholesale distribution channels over the next 5 years: (See Exhibit 2-2.)

- In 2006, 40% of wholesaler-distributors didn't share point-of-sale data with their suppliers. The wholesaler-distributors that did share point-of-sale data typically did so with only one to five suppliers.

- By 2012, almost 80% of wholesaler-distributors expect to be sharing point-of-sale data with up to 10 suppliers.

- We found similar penetration rates for other types of information sharing, such as wholesaler-distributors providing information on their product inventory levels to their suppliers.

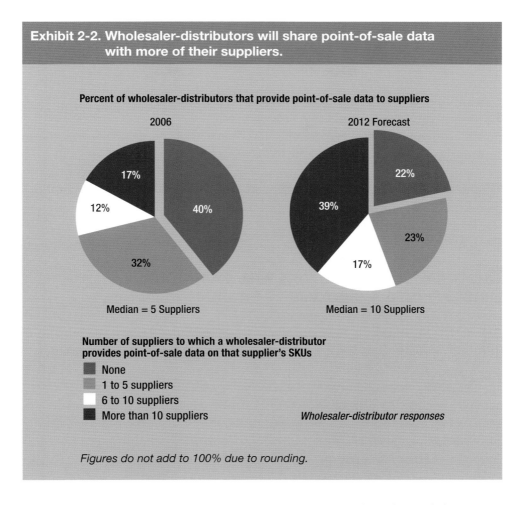

Exhibit 2-2. Wholesaler-distributors will share point-of-sale data with more of their suppliers.

Percent of wholesaler-distributors that provide point-of-sale data to suppliers

2006

17%
12%
40%
32%

Median = 5 Suppliers

2012 Forecast

22%
39%
23%
17%

Median = 10 Suppliers

Number of suppliers to which a wholesaler-distributor provides point-of-sale data on that supplier's SKUs

- None
- 1 to 5 suppliers
- 6 to 10 suppliers
- More than 10 suppliers

Wholesaler-distributor responses

Figures do not add to 100% due to rounding.

Most wholesaler-distributors are reluctant to collect and share demand data because they are suspicious that manufacturers will attempt to bypass the wholesale distribution channel. Few distributors wield as much channel power as retailers such as Wal-Mart, and this makes some distribution executives feel much more vulnerable about sharing point-of-sale data. Even so, the current and forecast prevalence of data sharing poses a challenge to this conventional wisdom.

However, customers' buying preferences somewhat limit the risk of data sharing. For example, wholesaler-distributors in the building materials and contractor supplies market (Chapter Six) maintain local inventory and sales resources to service market demand, as well as carry credit for smaller, often slow-paying contractors. Few manufacturers want to sell directly to these high-service customers.

The EDI transaction set 867 (Product Transfer and Resale Report) is the foundation of point-of-sale data sharing. EDI 867 can be used by wholesaler-distributors to report the following information to manufacturers:

- Sales of products from one or more locations to an end customer
- Demand beyond actual sales (lost orders)
- Product movement between locations of the same wholesale distribution company, such as products transferred from one branch to another.

Some lines of trade are proactively developing implementation standards for this transaction within their own industry channel, as we describe in the Action Ideas section of this chapter.

WHOLESALER-DISTRIBUTORS WILL GAIN MORE VISIBILITY INTO A CUSTOMER'S PRODUCT USAGE

VMI relationships allow a wholesaler-distributor to gain visibility about a customer's actual usage rather than just seeing a customer's orders. VMI refers to the practice of making an upstream supplier responsible for determining order size and timing by a downstream customer. For example, a wholesaler-distributor receives electronic data about a customer's sales and inventory stock levels. The wholesaler-distributor is then responsible for creating and maintaining the proper level of inventory. Under VMI, the distributor, not the customer, generates the order.

VMI is already used by almost one-third of wholesaler-distributors, although its use is expected to double over the next 5 years. (See Exhibit 2-3.) The greatest use of VMI occurs with customers operating from a fixed location, such as a manufacturing plant or retail store, versus customers operating at different job locations on different days, such as contractors.

Traditionally, the application of VMI is perceived to be much more limited with small contractors because they have short purchasing horizons geared toward the current job and day's work. Contractors often need materials right away for pickup or same-day delivery. However, the Action Ideas section at the end of this chapter highlights an innovative wholesaler-distributor that is already extending the VMI concept to plumbing contractors.

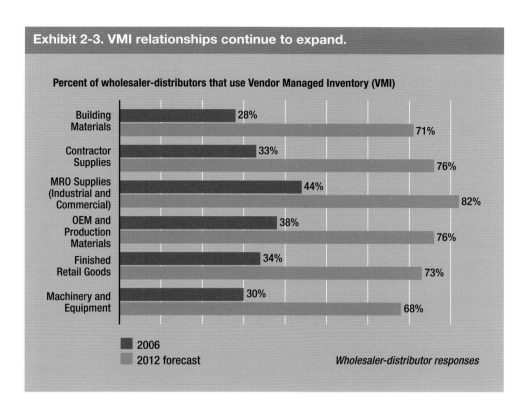

Exhibit 2-3. VMI relationships continue to expand.

Percent of wholesaler-distributors that use Vendor Managed Inventory (VMI)

Building Materials: 28% / 71%
Contractor Supplies: 33% / 76%
MRO Supplies (Industrial and Commercial): 44% / 82%
OEM and Production Materials: 38% / 76%
Finished Retail Goods: 34% / 73%
Machinery and Equipment: 30% / 68%

■ 2006
■ 2012 forecast   *Wholesaler-distributor responses*

Note that traditional VMI systems do not require transmission of EDI 867 documents. Instead, these systems rely on transmission of the related EDI transaction set 852 (Product Activity Report), which contains inventory levels and changes in product activity, such as the volume of products sold. However, product activity is reported as a single data point without regard to where the product is moving. Product activity is useful for determining restocking levels under a VMI relationship, but it is not sufficient to provide true point-of-sale data between a manufacturer-supplier and its wholesaler-distributor.

Despite the increased use of VMI, surprisingly few distributors rely on demand-based data when making inventory buying decisions. *Achieving Effective Inventory Management* by NAW/DREF found that 70% of wholesale distribution buyers forecast future purchases using relatively simple mathematical extrapolations of past demand.[10] The remaining 30% did no forecasting at all or just looked at the number of times the product was sold. Few buyers reported using the forecasting tools already available in their current technology systems.

WHOLESALER-DISTRIBUTORS WILL ADOPT AUTOMATIC PRODUCT IDENTIFICATION TECHNOLOGIES

Wholesaler-distributors will invest in the technology tools that enable product visibility in a demand-driven channel. These core technologies include a warehouse management system (WMS) combined with an automatic product identification system, such as a machine-readable bar code or a radio frequency identification (RFID) tag. Exhibit 2-4 shows the overall adoption rates for these three technologies for all wholesaler-distributors in this study.

Warehouse Management Systems (WMS)

WMS has been called the "brains of the warehouse"[11] because all decisions about the movement of products and people can be automated. In the warehouse, the productivity improvements of WMS come from substituting technology for potentially error-prone human activities, such as order processing, inventory control, and picking. For example, information sent from either handheld or fixed scanners creates real-time stock information and eliminates the need for manual inventory counting. As with many technologies, adoption has lagged among smaller wholesaler-distributors.

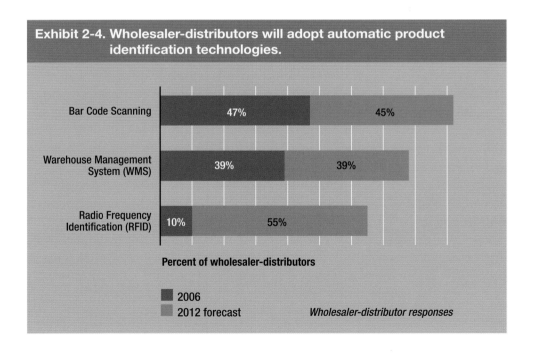

Exhibit 2-4. Wholesaler-distributors will adopt automatic product identification technologies.

Bar Code Scanning: 47% (2006), 45% (2012 forecast)
Warehouse Management System (WMS): 39% (2006), 39% (2012 forecast)
Radio Frequency Identification (RFID): 10% (2006), 55% (2012 forecast)

Percent of wholesaler-distributors

■ 2006
■ 2012 forecast

Wholesaler-distributor responses

Bar Codes

Bar codes have proved to be a highly accurate method for identifying products, with most errors tied to human failures in scanning the machine-readable tags. Adoption of this legacy technology remains surprisingly low among small and midsized wholesaler-distributors. Fewer than two out of five wholesaler-distributors with revenues below $20 million used bar codes in 2006, although most plan to implement bar codes by 2012. Suppliers will be increasing their use of bar codes on products shipped to their wholesaler-distributors at all levels of product aggregation (pallet, case, and individual item). (See Exhibit 2-5.)

Radio Frequency Identification (RFID)

RFID does not have the line-of-sight scanning requirements of bar codes and this reduces physical handling. In theory, items can be uniquely identified and tracked through the entire supply chain without ever being physically scanned. In our survey, only 10% of wholesaler-distributors were using RFID in 2006, while 65% expect to be using the technology within 5 years. (See Exhibit 2-4.)

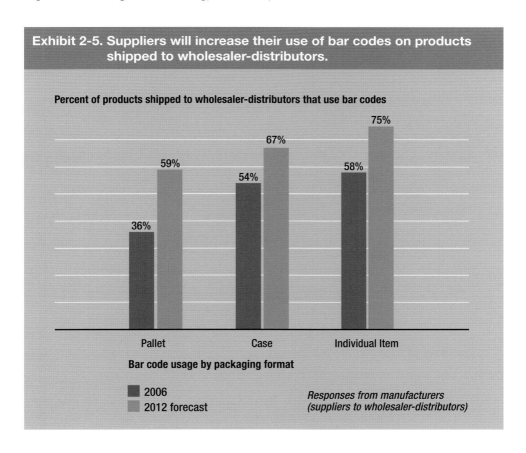

Exhibit 2-5. Suppliers will increase their use of bar codes on products shipped to wholesaler-distributors.

Percent of products shipped to wholesaler-distributors that use bar codes

Bar code usage by packaging format

- 2006
- 2012 forecast

Responses from manufacturers (suppliers to wholesaler-distributors)

RFID was identified as an emerging technology in the 2004 report and continued in 2006 to be viewed as an important supply chain technology. Actual RFID market growth has not met the projections cited in the 2004 report, although there have been some reported successes. For instance, Wal-Mart announced in 2003 that it would require all of its suppliers to embed RFID tags in all cases and pallets by 2006. This mandate was modified in 2005 to include only Wal-Mart's top 100 suppliers; some reports indicate that many suppliers are only using RFID on pallets.

As our 2004 report pointed out, wholesaler-distributors should remain wary of the RFID hype, given the ongoing uncertainty about technological feasibility, costs, and the willingness of supply chain partners to embrace this technology. The positive expectations for RFID in Exhibit 2-4 may also reflect the fact that this research surveyed senior wholesale distribution executives rather than warehouse managers. For example, one study of warehouse operations managers found that 64% of warehouses had no plans to implement RFID.[12]

To date, the benefits of RFID appear to be greatest when used within a single company on specific projects. For example, independent research by researchers at the University of Arkansas found that RFID reduced stock outs in Wal-Mart stores by 30% by improving shelf replenishment from the backroom to store shelves.[13] Other common applications of RFID technology within a single company include using tags to track tools, expensive equipment, and frequently stolen items.

Regardless of the product identification technology uses, wireless technologies will increasingly be the basis for transmitting data from the warehouse floor into the business system, rather than manually recording and entering information into the system later. Similarly, wireless voice-directed systems can also reduce human-picking errors by pointing warehouse employees to the right location and quantities. Wireless systems also change both the cost and usefulness of warehouse automation by allowing a distributor to achieve the benefits of new systems within an existing warehouse configuration.

MANUFACTURER STRATEGIES WILL HOLD BACK
DEMAND-DRIVEN CHANNELS IN SOME LINES OF TRADE

Market share is a key measure of success for manufacturers, just as service levels are critical for distributors. While the conceptual and financial appeal of a demand-driven channel seems apparent, many manufacturers push back because of the overriding importance of market share over supply chain efficiencies to manufacturers.[14]

Manufacturers must keep their factories operating near capacity to cover the fixed costs associated with plant, equipment, and employees. Manufacturers build new facilities or overhaul existing plants when launching new products. Funding these capital expenditures requires both time and money. Market share will pay for investments and keep competitors at bay.

Competitive manufacturers are working simultaneously to keep their factories running at full capacity and grow their business by taking away customers from their competitors. This takes significant overhead, which is measured in research and development, sales, advertising, branding, and other expenses. Maintaining or growing market share means that a manufacturer is denying the oxygen needed by its competitors. The best market share strategies keep competitors from ever establishing a critical mass that is needed to be a formidable opponent.

Wholesaler-distributors face similar overhead pressures, but they can usually add new products or brands when others decline. Wholesaler-distributors also have fewer fixed costs because personnel and warehouse space can be added or subtracted in much smaller increments than a large manufacturing plant investment. Distributors' reputations are built on service levels and they do not lose credibility when a customer switches brands.

Ironically, a relentless focus on market share by manufacturers opens the door to private label strategies by wholesaler-distributors as outlined in Chapter One. Customers may look for wholesaler-distributors to incorporate product manufacturing as a way to enhance supply chain efficiencies if upstream manufacturers are not willing to sufficiently restructure their operations.

Now that we've looked closely at the demand-driven channels trend, let's look at specific strategies within the following Action Ideas to help you better understand the implications of this trend for your company. This chapter closes with Questions for Management Discussion that you and your team can tackle right away.

ACTION IDEAS

1. Support appropriate implementation standards for your line of trade.

The importance of wholesale distribution in many lines of trade should encourage distribution executives to get involved in the development of appropriate standards. This will ensure that any requirements reflect the real-world complexity and technology capabilities of wholesaler-distributors.

For example, a task force of manufacturing and distribution executives in the electrical products industry outlined the benefits and opportunities of sharing point-of-sale data.[15] The task force concluded: "...sharing information with channel partners will allow the electrical distribution channel to develop new efficiencies and uncover new avenues of profitable growth."

The task force identified four specific benefits from sharing 867 data between trading partners:

1. Manufacturers and distributors can reap the benefits of a more demand-driven channel, such as lower lead times, better fill rates, and increased inventory turns.

2. Manufacturers and distributors can use the data for fact-based joint planning, especially when the data are provided with industry coding information.

3. Manufacturers can more accurately assign sales credit to their salesforces.

4. Manufacturers can provide distributors with category management guidelines to help distributors stock and inventory a more profitable mix of products.

The electrical industry benefits from its own standards organization called the **Industry Data Exchange Association** (IDEA, www.idea-esolutions.com). The National Electrical Manufacturers Association and the National Association of Electrical Distributors created IDEA jointly in 1998 to create electronic catalog content at an industry level. IDEA has created an electronic standard for the submission of 867 data in multiple electronic formats, such as traditional EDI, flat file, and Excel spreadsheet.

2. Require appropriate rewards for sharing point-of-sale data.

Wholesaler-distributors should recognize that point-of-sale data provide value to a supplier. Therefore, the distributor should be offered, or should ask for, some form of direct or indirect reward for sharing these data. Point-of-sale data represent one example of how channel compensation from manufacturers is becoming a more important source of gross margin for wholesaler-distributors, and this is a topic that we discuss further in Chapter Three.

C.H. Briggs Hardware Co. (www.chbriggs.com), a large, independently owned building materials distributor, began sharing point-of-sale data with one of its key suppliers in 2005. The supplier approached C.H. Briggs in order to understand which customers were buying its products and the gross margins received by its distributors for different types of customers. C.H. Briggs now provides monthly point-of-sale data using a flat file version of the EDI 867 standard. In exchange for providing the data, C.H. Briggs receives the following mix of direct and indirect compensation:

- A product price discount for transacting via EDI
- An additional product price discount for sharing point-of-sale data
- Specific cross-selling ideas from the supplier derived from data aggregated across multiple distributors
- Additional field sales and technical support from the supplier provided on joint customer calls.

The company's managers estimate that the cross-selling data and field sales support provide a bigger benefit than the product price discount. Since beginning the program, C.H. Briggs has been able to increase its sales of the supplier's products by more than 25%.

This example also highlights the collaborative nature of information sharing between manufacturers and distributors. Identifying new sales opportunities at existing accounts must be uncovered using fact-based insights drawn from customer-level data analytics. It can be extremely challenging and time consuming for all but the largest wholesaler-distributors to identify the right items for a cross-selling offer without access to a broader data set created from multiple companies. Both sides of the relationship gain business benefits from sharing point-of-sale data, thus providing a relevant counter example to the conventional wisdom described earlier in this chapter.

3. Apply demand-driven concepts to your business.

Distributors can take advantage of the demand-driven trend to build better forecasts, improve warehouse efficiency, and remain a preferred route to market for suppliers and customers. Some innovative wholesaler-distributors are already extending the VMI concept into new markets.

Barnett (www.e-barnett.com), a distributor of plumbing, HVAC, electrical, and hardware products to professional contractors, developed a creative truck inventory replenishment program that allows the company and its plumbing customers to take advantage of the demand-driven trend. A Barnett sales rep works with a plumbing contractor to create a standard truck stock list for each service truck. After the plumbing contractor completes a job, he/she notes the parts used on an order sheet or scans the appropriate bar code using a Barnett-provided inventory scanner. Orders are transmitted electronically to Barnett at the end of each workday, and this provides an almost real-time view of end customer demand. Barnett then ships by truck replenishment inventory.

By gathering point-of-use information electronically, Barnett is able to optimize its inventory levels, increase service levels, grow sales per customers, and build strong customer loyalty. The plumbing contractor benefits from more accurate truck restocking, lower warehouse labor costs, and dramatically reduced inventory carrying costs.

Demand-based forecasts allow a distributor to ensure that the right products are in stock at the right time and in the right quantities. Buying correctly increases operating cash flows by reducing excess inventory investments. Fewer out-of-date or obsolete products will remain in the warehouse, so that less inventory is eventually written off.

QUESTIONS FOR MANAGEMENT DISCUSSION

Here are discussion questions for your management team. Please review the detailed results for your specific customers and markets in Chapters Six through Eight before discussing these topics.

1. Which of the following factors cause the variability in our orders to suppliers to become much greater than the variability in actual usage by our customers?

   • Aggressive volume discounts that encourage us to place very large orders
   • Long lead times and/or poor service levels from suppliers that encourage us to build excess safety stock
   • Little visibility into our customers' actual usage versus just seeing customer orders
   • Overly high order minimums that encourage our customers to delay their orders, thereby shielding us from their actual usage patterns

2. What is the financial impact on our company from bullwhip effects within our line of trade? Possible areas of impact include:

   • Reduced cash flow due to excessive investment in inventory
   • Depressed service levels due to incorrect inventory investments
   • Higher operating costs from higher product handling or warehouse expenses.

3. What is the business value of point-of-sale data to our key suppliers? What level of direct or indirect compensation would be acceptable to our company for sharing these data?

4. Discuss the pros and cons of sharing point-of-sale or product movement data with our key suppliers. What are the biggest issues and barriers?

   • No interest by our suppliers
   • Lack of trust in how our suppliers will use our data
   • Inadequate compensation from our suppliers

   Does our data-sharing agreement with suppliers address data ownership and the proper use of the data? How can we minimize the risks of sharing data with suppliers?

5. Where is our company relative to our competitors on the adoption of automatic product identification technologies? Where are we missing opportunities to improve the productivity of our warehouse and physical handling operations?

CHAPTER THREE

New Profit Models

SUMMARY

Manufacturers will increase their share of a wholesaler-distributor's profit margin from product distribution, and this will lead to greater use of pay-for-performance channel compensation models by manufacturers. Wholesaler-distributors will need to understand whether their companies are truly profitable channel partners. Nevertheless, wholesaler-distributors can benefit from better measurement of performance and can derive new profit streams in the supply chain. New compensation methods that will grow in importance include fee-for-service payments from customers, discounts from suppliers based on the performance of specified activities, and fee-for-service payments from suppliers. For example, some distributors provide outsourced fulfillment as a fee-based service to traditional suppliers, thereby beating back the threat from logistics companies. Others have successfully created new profit models through fee-based services to customers, which will keep growing across most wholesale distribution industry segments.

Ongoing success will require wholesaler-distributors to master the financial dynamics of a services business, which are different from those of a product distribution business. Wholesaler-distributors will also need to monitor new developments at competing logistics companies and avoid overconfidence in the unique value of their own logistics prowess.

Data Points

- About 91% of manufacturers expect to stop doing business with highly unprofitable wholesaler-distributors by 2012.
- Approximately 52% of manufacturers expect to be paying fees to their wholesaler-distributors for product delivery to a customer account.
- More than 75% of wholesaler-distributors expect to offer fee-based services to customers or suppliers within 5 years.

WHOLESALER-DISTRIBUTORS WILL GENERATE MORE OF THEIR MARGINS FROM SUPPLIERS

A wholesaler-distributor's gross margin comes from two sources. First, manufacturers set prices or provide buy-side incentives and discounts that allow a distributor to earn a margin. Second, customers pay a sell-side markup above the cost of the products, thus reflecting the value of the channel. Support and other services are included in the price paid by the customer.

This traditional mix will change as customers negotiate harder with wholesaler-distributors, essentially reducing the amount they are willing to pay for a wholesaler-distributor's services. As we discuss in Chapter Four, customers will also question the value added by wholesaler-distributors due to the ready availability of online information and more sophisticated sourcing techniques. Customers' growing power will allow them to require wholesale distribution suppliers to provide new services without any additional margin or fee compensation. (See Exhibit 3-1.) Large volume buyers will demand ever-deeper discounts from wholesaler-distributors to secure their business and this will lead to intense competition among the largest wholesalers and sell-side margin pressure. Distributors of machinery and equipment products will be partially sheltered from this trend, perhaps due to the prevalence of maintenance and service requirements after a capital equipment purchase.

In response, manufacturers will become more important to a wholesaler-distributor's profit margin from product distribution. Exhibit 3-2 shows eight possible sources of gross margin for a wholesaler-distributor. Four of the five compensation methods, which are expected to increase most in importance, derive from manufacturers rather than customers. They are

- Discounts from suppliers based on the performance of specified activities
- Supplier rebates based on total purchases in a specified time period
- Discounts from suppliers based on purchase volume
- Fee-for-service payments from suppliers.

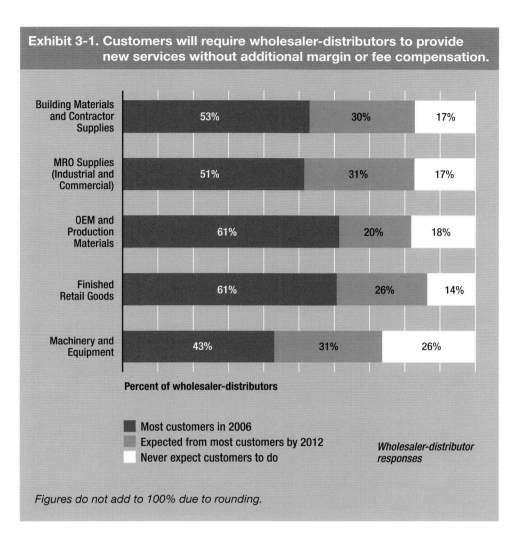

Exhibit 3-1. Customers will require wholesaler-distributors to provide new services without additional margin or fee compensation.

Building Materials and Contractor Supplies	53%	30%	17%
MRO Supplies (Industrial and Commercial)	51%	31%	17%
OEM and Production Materials	61%	20%	18%
Finished Retail Goods	61%	26%	14%
Machinery and Equipment	43%	31%	26%

Percent of wholesaler-distributors

■ Most customers in 2006
■ Expected from most customers by 2012
□ Never expect customers to do

Wholesaler-distributor responses

Figures do not add to 100% due to rounding.

Product markups to customers and the ability to purchase at a wholesale discount will remain important to wholesaler-distributors' gross margin, while fee-for-service payments from customers will become much more important. Most wholesaler-distributors expect traditional sources of profit, such as wholesaler discounts or forward buying in advance of a price increase, to also remain relevant to their profitability in the future.

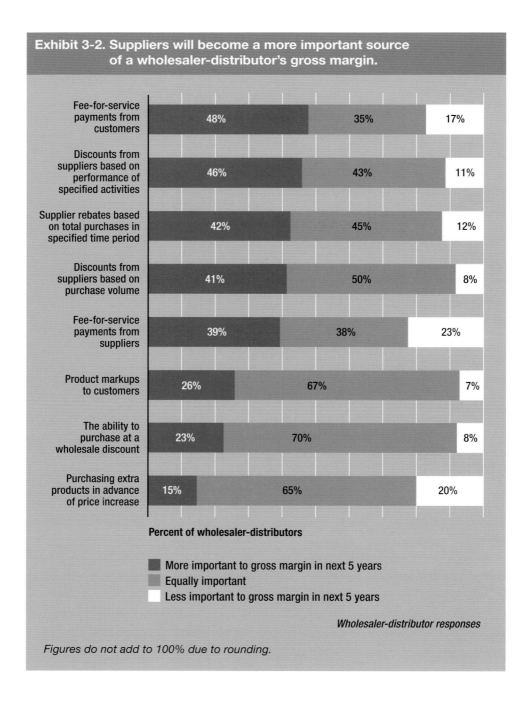

Exhibit 3-2. Suppliers will become a more important source of a wholesaler-distributor's gross margin.

Source	More important	Equally important	Less important
Fee-for-service payments from customers	48%	35%	17%
Discounts from suppliers based on performance of specified activities	46%	43%	11%
Supplier rebates based on total purchases in specified time period	42%	45%	12%
Discounts from suppliers based on purchase volume	41%	50%	8%
Fee-for-service payments from suppliers	39%	38%	23%
Product markups to customers	26%	67%	7%
The ability to purchase at a wholesale discount	23%	70%	8%
Purchasing extra products in advance of price increase	15%	65%	20%

Percent of wholesaler-distributors

■ More important to gross margin in next 5 years
■ Equally important
□ Less important to gross margin in next 5 years

Wholesaler-distributor responses

Figures do not add to 100% due to rounding.

CHANNEL COMPENSATION WILL MIGRATE TO PAY-FOR-PERFORMANCE MODELS

As suppliers gain more control over compensation, wholesaler-distributors face a future of greater accountability for their activities and results. Our survey of manufacturers supplying to wholesaler-distributors found the following clear intentions that they will subject their distributors to greater scrutiny and hold them more accountable:

- Slightly more than one-half (52%) of manufacturer-suppliers stopped working with highly unprofitable wholesaler-distributors in 2006.

- About 91% of manufacturer-suppliers expect to stop doing business with highly unprofitable wholesaler-distributors by 2012.

In other words, these suppliers intend to evaluate a wholesaler-distributor based on more than just total sales volume. Surprisingly, these results did not differ by the revenue size of a supplier, the major type of products manufactured, or the total number of wholesaler-distributors carrying the product.

Channel compensation programs by manufacturer-suppliers represent a powerful tool by which manufacturers can motivate the wholesaler-distributors within their channel. These programs work because price discounts, rebates, fees, and marketing funds provide economic incentives that get the attention of wholesaler-distributors and reward results. There are two general models for linking a wholesaler-distributor's compensation more closely to specific outcomes:

- **Functional discounts.** The manufacturer-supplier provides a basic discount available to the wholesale distribution channel, plus a list of additional discounts off of the list price that are available in return for performing specific channel functions. Typical functions might include paying promptly to the supplier, penetrating a new market or segment, and maintaining a certain level of inventory. In other words, this structure breaks the traditional supplier discount to a wholesaler-distributor into discrete components that are matched to discrete activities. Wholesaler-distributors that perform all functions will often earn the same discount, while distributors performing only a subset of functions will get a portion of the total discount.

- **Fee-for-service.** The manufacturer-supplier separates product costs from distribution costs by paying directly for the activities performed by a wholesaler-distributor. Unlike functional discounts, the compensation to a wholesaler-distributor is not based on a discount off of the product list price. Manufacturers can customize the precise support activities, while distributors earn fees commensurate with their effort, costs, and results.

As Exhibit 3-2 demonstrates, both models will increase in importance over the next 5 years. These models can often coexist in the same industry because different manufacturers choose alternative approaches. A manufacturer can use these programs to resolve conflict among different types of wholesaler-distributors in its network if customers can divide their research and purchase activities. This can occur when customers gather product information from a wholesaler-distributor that provides extensive prepurchase support, but then purchase through a low-cost channel that provides no information or support. A larger functional discount or a fee-based payment will support additional prepurchase activities for the higher-service wholesaler-distributor.

Some wholesaler-distributors will welcome this scrutiny. An executive at an electrical and plumbing distributor said: "It is very important for suppliers to look seriously at developing their people and putting into place a structured development plan to prepare for the changing dynamic of the wholesaler-distributor. It will soon not be about selling widgets, but about services and value to the supply chain."

DEMAND-DRIVEN CHANNELS WILL ENABLE PAY-FOR-PERFORMANCE MODELS

Wholesaler-distributors' compensation will be more directly linked to outcomes as manufacturers' visibility of downstream channel activity increases. New performance metrics become possible once suppliers gain visibility into channel activities and this allows for better measurements of wholesaler-distributors' performance.

Wholesaler-distributors that share data with suppliers are also more likely to use pay-for-performance models. Evidence of the link between pay-for-performance and data sharing comes from comparing the expectations of wholesaler-distributors currently sharing point-of-sale data (as described in Chapter Two) with wholesaler-distributors that are not sharing these data. Wholesale distribution executives whose companies share data believe the two relevant compensation approaches from Exhibit 3-3—fee-for-service and functional compensation—will become much more important to gross margins. In other words, wholesale distribution executives at companies already sharing some data have more experience operating in a higher visibility (pay-for-performance) environment.

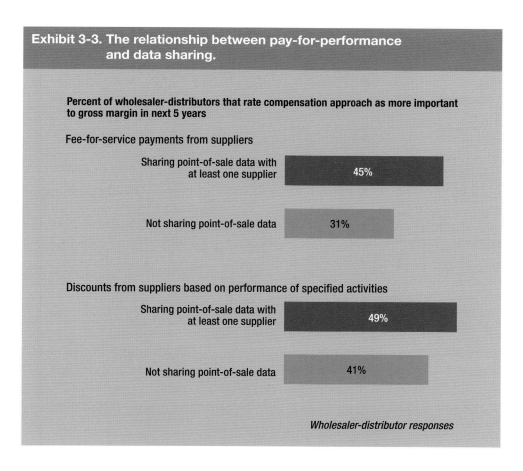

Exhibit 3-3. The relationship between pay-for-performance and data sharing.

Percent of wholesaler-distributors that rate compensation approach as more important to gross margin in next 5 years

Fee-for-service payments from suppliers

Sharing point-of-sale data with at least one supplier — 45%

Not sharing point-of-sale data — 31%

Discounts from suppliers based on performance of specified activities

Sharing point-of-sale data with at least one supplier — 49%

Not sharing point-of-sale data — 41%

Wholesaler-distributor responses

No industry channel has moved farther down the pay-for-performance path than the wholesale distribution of pharmaceutical products.[16] Until 2002, most drug manufacturers compensated wholesalers such as **AmerisourceBergen** (www.amerisourcebergen.com), **Cardinal Health** (www.cardinal.com), and **McKesson Corporation** (www.mckesson.com) by allowing them to purchase more products than near-term sales demand required. Since drug prices were increasing, wholesaler-distributors could earn as much as 40% profit of their gross margin by holding extra inventory and selling it when prices increased.

Unfortunately, manufacturers found themselves unable to control the activities of their distribution channels. Wholesalers made money as speculators rather than as product distributors. Thousands of small wholesalers sprung up to buy and sell the excess channel inventory in a virtually unregulated secondary market. This created opportunities for unscrupulous parties to introduce counterfeit or mishandled products into the U.S. drug distribution system. Neither manufacturers nor wholesalers had clear incentives to lower inventory levels in the supply chain.

Channel relationships were transformed only after manufacturers and distributors began signing new distribution agreements in 2003. Since 2006, manufacturers are successfully paying U.S. wholesalers not to hold more than 1 month of inventory. Most arrangements offer some form of performance benefit to help distributors offset profits they have lost by discontinuing inventory investment. For example, wholesaler-distributors can receive higher payments for making more accurate forecasts of their orders to suppliers. In some agreements, fee-for-service payments are directly linked to various metrics that ensure a wholesaler is shipping to customer orders and not merely building stock.

As a result of these new business arrangements, the inventory-to-sales ratio in the wholesaler-distributor channel has declined by 50% in the past 4 years, even while total wholesaler sales have grown by one-third. Wholesalers have avoided adding an incremental $7.5 billion of inventory to their balance sheets. Although manufacturers removed investment-buying profits, wholesalers' operating cash flows are soaring substantially as they reduce inventory investments.

Consistent with the trend identified in Chapter Two, the new compensation models are enabled by new technology linkages between supply chain partners. Pharmaceutical wholesalers continuously share order, inventory-to-sales, and shipment data with manufacturers via EDI transaction sets. Manufacturers use real-time analyses of these data to evaluate wholesaler orders, balance inventory-to-sales levels in the channel, prevent leakages into the secondary market, manage service fill rates, limit unauthorized distribution, and compensate wholesaler-distributors for accurate and complete reporting.

WHOLESALER-DISTRIBUTORS WILL EMERGE AS THE PREFERRED FEE-FOR-SERVICE LOGISTICS PROVIDERS

As predicted in the 2004 report, wholesaler-distributors are increasingly offering logistics and outsourced fulfillment as a fee-based service to traditional suppliers.

Our research found that 29% of manufacturers pay one or more of their wholesaler-distributors to deliver products to a customer account for a fee. In the future, 52% of manufacturers expect to be paying these fees. Manufacturers selling OEM products or finished retail goods are more likely to pay a fee to a wholesaler-distributor for product delivery to a customer account. These arrangements appear to be more likely when a few large end customers seek a direct relationship with a manufacturer, but the manufacturer needs the wholesale distribution channels to service a critical mass of smaller customers that cannot be served directly.

One approach for a wholesaler-distributor involves splitting physical logistics and fulfillment from sales and marketing. Two separate business units—one for the logistics division and one for traditional wholesale distribution—coexist within the same parent company. The objective is to leverage technology, warehouse infrastructure, and logistics to support suppliers without performing sales and marketing activities. Since the publication of our 2004 report, this strategy has become much more common in wholesale distribution.

For example, **Avnet** (www.avnet.com), one of the two largest distributors in the electronic components industry, launched **Avnet Logistics** (logistics.avnet.com) in October 2004. The logistics division operates as a third-party logistics company by providing supply chain consulting and logistics execution services to global electronic components suppliers. Unlike logistics companies without a distributor heritage, Avnet Logistics is able to build on the parent company's knowledge of the electronics industry in areas such as product allocations, supplier relationships, and environmental regulations.

The two divisions can succeed because the electronic components industry supports both large and small customers. The top 10 global technology products manufacturers and contract manufacturing companies purchase large volumes of semiconductors and other electronic components. These customers are increasingly unwilling to pay for the selling infrastructure of a wholesale distribution channel, especially when they perceive the traditional channel adds little value to sales and marketing. However, these products are also purchased by thousands of small- and medium-sized value-added resellers, systems builders, systems integrators, and other buyers. Since product manufacturers are unable to serve these customers cost effectively, this makes wholesale distribution the most significant route to market for this customer base.

An alternate strategy involves keeping the logistics operations integrated within the core wholesale distribution organization. This is more likely the case when products require industry-specific knowledge and particular handling cannot be taken over easily by a nonspecialist logistics provider.

Consider the distribution channels for products such as wood flooring or pet food. These products require specialized handling and also have a low value-to-weight ratio, which makes them less attractive to a generalist logistics company.

Smaller customers coexist with big-box retailers to sell these products and this creates a bifurcated structure in which wholesaler-distributors remain relevant. For example, floor covering retailing remains one of the most fragmented retail sectors with more than 15,000 stores operating in the United States. Similarly, more than 8,000 pet food stores remain despite the growth of large retailers such as **Petco** (www.petco.com) and **Petsmart** (www.petsmart.com).

However, the large, multiple-location retailers have centralized purchasing systems and in-house distribution capabilities. The large buyers do not want to purchase through a geographically dispersed network of independent wholesaler-distributors because doing so would limit purchasing volume discounts and expose retailers to multiple technology systems and regional pricing variations.

Rather than establish separate logistics subsidiaries, the wholesaler-distributors deliver products on behalf of suppliers to the individual stores of a large customer account. The manufacturer that receives orders directly from the retailer handles national account management. However, fulfillment is done by an independent wholesaler-distributor. The distributor's compensation is typically a fee paid by the supplier, thus making this a form of fee-for-service payment. (See Exhibit 3-2.) Although not operating as a logistics subsidiary, the manufacturer still sells directly to the national account but pays a fee to distributors for local fulfillment service.

LOGISTICS COMPANIES WILL STRUGGLE TO COMPETE WITH WHOLESALER-DISTRIBUTORS

The fee-for-service logistics strategies being used by wholesaler-distributors have tempered manufacturers' enthusiasm for using logistics companies as viable alternatives to wholesaler-distributors for core activities. The past 3 years have not noticeably advanced the perceived competitiveness of logistics providers compared to results found in the 2004 report. (See Exhibit 3-4.) Distributors still retain a distinct advantage in postsales service and support.

For example, *The 10th Annual Third-Party Logistics Study*,[17] which surveyed more than 1,000 users of logistics services, found users were often disappointed with third-party logistics providers' ability to develop advanced services. Many third-party logistics providers apparently satisfy user requirements around basic services such as transportation and warehousing. However, logistics providers lagged behind customer expectations in developing more advanced capabilities such as inventory-based services, contract manufacturing, broad business process outsourcing, and/or technology innovation.

Logistics companies will continue to challenge wholesale distribution's core logistics and fulfillment functions. However, many wholesaler-distributors of all sizes plan to compete directly with logistics companies by offering logistics as a fee-based service. (See Exhibit 3-5.) This will make it harder than originally forecasted to displace the wholesale distribution channel functions.

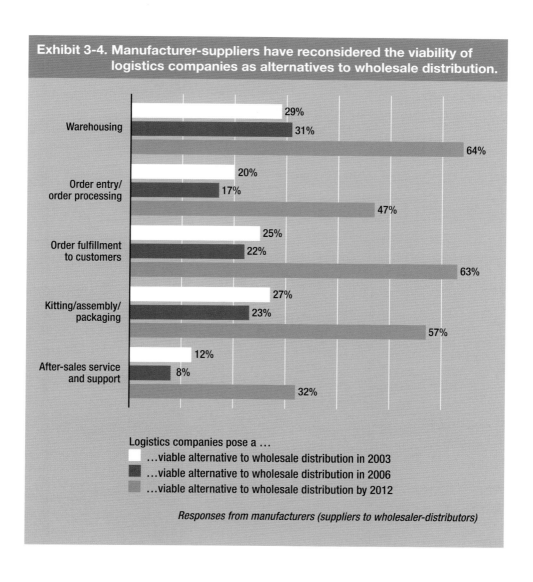

Exhibit 3-4. Manufacturer-suppliers have reconsidered the viability of logistics companies as alternatives to wholesale distribution.

Warehousing
29%
31%
64%

Order entry/ order processing
20%
17%
47%

Order fulfillment to customers
25%
22%
63%

Kitting/assembly/ packaging
27%
23%
57%

After-sales service and support
12%
8%
32%

Logistics companies pose a ...
☐ ...viable alternative to wholesale distribution in 2003
■ ...viable alternative to wholesale distribution in 2006
▨ ...viable alternative to wholesale distribution by 2012

Responses from manufacturers (suppliers to wholesaler-distributors)

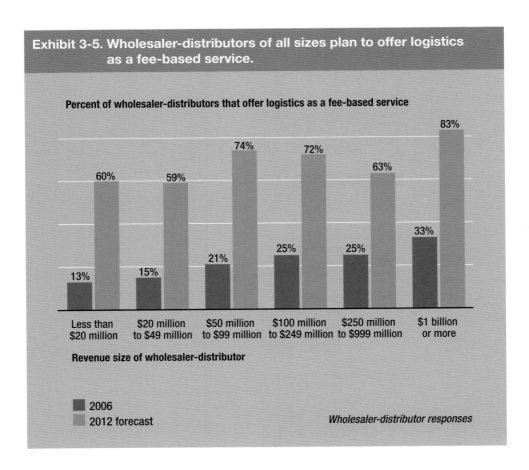

Exhibit 3-5. Wholesaler-distributors of all sizes plan to offer logistics as a fee-based service.

Percent of wholesaler-distributors that offer logistics as a fee-based service

Revenue size	2006	2012 forecast
Less than $20 million	13%	60%
$20 million to $49 million	15%	59%
$50 million to $99 million	21%	74%
$100 million to $249 million	25%	72%
$250 million to $999 million	25%	63%
$1 billion or more	33%	83%

Revenue size of wholesaler-distributor

■ 2006
■ 2012 forecast

Wholesaler-distributor responses

FEE-BASED SERVICES FROM WHOLESALER-DISTRIBUTORS WILL KEEP GROWING

In the 2004 report, we forecasted that wholesaler-distributors would charge fees for their services rather than merely give away *value added* and hope to recoup the costs with product margins. Since 2006, many wholesaler-distributors are successfully selling fee-based services, thereby positioning themselves as suppliers of products with related services instead of only reliably providing goods. The skepticism shown toward fee-based services in our 2001 study *Facing the Forces of Change®: Future Scenarios for Wholesale Distribution* has now been firmly replaced by real-world success.

While a critical mass of wholesaler-distributors across all industry segments were offering fee-based services in 2006, more than 75% expect to offer fee-based services within 5 years. (See Exhibit 3-6.)

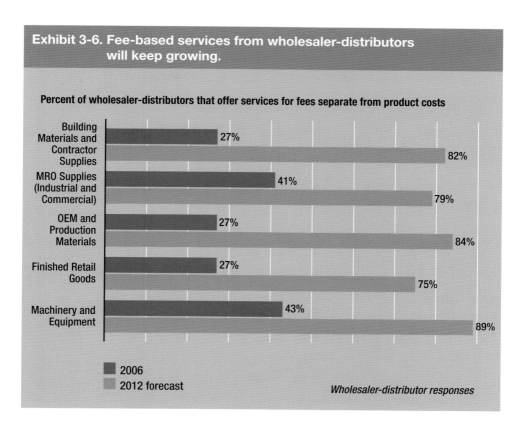

Exhibit 3-6. Fee-based services from wholesaler-distributors will keep growing.

Percent of wholesaler-distributors that offer services for fees separate from product costs

Category	2006	2012 forecast
Building Materials and Contractor Supplies	27%	82%
MRO Supplies (Industrial and Commercial)	41%	79%
OEM and Production Materials	27%	84%
Finished Retail Goods	27%	75%
Machinery and Equipment	43%	89%

■ 2006
■ 2012 forecast

Wholesaler-distributor responses

Fee-based services must directly improve a customer's profitability and operations by providing specific, measurable gains in its business. Success is not measured by delivery times or fill rates, but rather by customer productivity gains, labor savings, ergonomic improvements, and a faster time-to-market. Fee-based services change the customer-distributor relationship by forcing distributors to deliver specific, measurable results, as well as maintain excellence in their core activities.

Consider **Bryan Equipment Sales, Inc.** (www.bryanequipment.com), a distributor of outdoor power equipment tools to full-servicing retailers such as contractor/supply houses, lawn equipment dealers, and hardware stores. In addition to traditional product distribution, Bryan installs in-store merchandising systems as a fee-based service for its retail dealer customers, most of which are usually smaller businesses that appreciate the personalized merchandizing expertise. The company uses a crew of five installers to deliver and maintain the systems.

Exhibit 3-7 provides representative examples of other fee-based services being offered by wholesaler-distributors of all sizes and across many lines of trade. In each case, a wholesaler-distributor has developed a service that improves the customer's

Exhibit 3-7. Examples of successful fee-based services from wholesaler-distributors.

Company	Web Site	Major Product Lines	Successful Fee-Based Service Examples
Bryan Equipment Sales	www.bryanequipment.com	Outdoor Power Equipment	Dealer merchandising systems
D&D Tool & Supply	www.ddtool.com	Tooling Products and MRO Industrial Supplies	Tool room management
Eastway Supplies	www.eastwaysupplies.com	Plumbing, Heating, Cooling, Piping (PHCP) Products	Installation of shower doors and mirrors
Gustave A. Larson Company	www.galarson.com	Heating, Ventilation, Air Conditioning, and Refrigeration (HVACR) Equipment, Parts and Supplies	Crane lift service for commercial rooftops, compressors, and pipe
H.D. Smith	www.hdsmith.com	Health Care Products	Business and marketing services for independent pharmacies
Industrial Distribution Group	www.idg-corp.com	MRO Supplies	Store room management
Kellermeyer	www.kellermeyer.com	Supplies, Cleaning Equipment, and Packaging Products	Equipment repairs
The Knotts Company	www.knottsco.com	Fluid Power and Industrial Automation	Construction of frames and machine elements
The Rowland Company	www.rowland2.com	Industrial Power Transmission Components	Fabrication and assembly
R.W. Smith & Co.	www.rwsmithco.com	Restaurant Equipment and Supplies	Design and development of restaurant kitchens
Safety Today	www.safetytoday.com	Personal Safety Products	Instrument repair
Stag-Parkway	www.stagparkway.com	RV Parts and Accessories	Print marketing collateral
Stanion Wholesale Electric Co.	www.stanion.com	Electrical Products	Technical training

business by taking on critical tasks. Distributors have been less successful when simply trying to charge for activities that used to be given away for free. The exceptions have been distributors that have been able to redevelop an old service so that it becomes different from the value-added services being offered *for free* by competitors.

Distributors have always been in an excellent position to capture the services revenues, although many have still not taken advantage of this opportunity. One of the biggest barriers can be the internal assumptions and beliefs of wholesale distribution management. Here are a few representative comments from wholesale distribution executives describing their biggest barriers in launching a fee-based service along with their companies' primary product lines:

- "We had to convince our own salespeople of the value of the service above and beyond the labor and parts costs." (automation controls)

- "It was difficult to get our customers and suppliers to accept us as a fee-based services provider given the fact that they all have known us for many years as a product distribution company and as a company that has bundled products and services." (electronic components)

- "Training the sales associates for consultative sell. Some of the sales associates will never be comfortable." (industrial MRO products)

- "Ourselves. For the longest time, we were sure we could not and should not charge our customers for training." (electrical products)

- "Culturally we always gave this away. It's amazing what we can charge with no questions asked!" (hydraulic and pneumatic products)

Now that we've looked closely at the new profit models trend, let's look at specific strategies within the following Action Ideas to help you better understand the implications of this trend for your company. This chapter closes with Questions for Management Discussion that you and your team can tackle right away.

ACTION IDEAS

1. Analyze whether you are a profitable channel partner.

As channel compensation becomes more fact-based and performance-oriented, this same analytic process will be used by suppliers to wholesaler-distributors in evaluating the relative profitability of their channel partners. Recall that 91% of manufacturer-suppliers expect to stop doing business with highly unprofitable wholesaler-distributors by 2012.

The evaluation of a wholesaler-distributor's profitability to a supplier is analogous to the process by which a wholesaler-distributor evaluates the profitability of its own customers. A supplier links expenses to individual wholesaler-distributors using an activity-based costing approach and then identifies the true operating profit of working with each of its channel partners. For example, with all other factors being equal, a wholesaler-distributor submitting EDI orders will be less costly to serve than one submitting faxed orders. Combining price and volume data generated from automated order streams with internal cost information from an enterprise resource planning (ERP) system enable these analyses.

Representative costs that a manufacturer might incur when doing business with an individual wholesaler-distributor include:

- Total promotional discounts and rebate payments
- Field sales expenses and commissions
- Co-op advertising and promotional spending
- Warehouse and handling costs based on product shipments
- Freight expenses
- Cost of handling returns
- Costs of capital for accounts receivable
- Customer service and order processing expenses
- Technical and sales support
- Allocated overhead such as brand advertising and administration.

Imagine a supplier asking the following two questions about the wholesale distribution companies that sell its products:

- Which of our wholesaler-distributors provide positive operating profits?
- Which of our wholesaler-distributors have the greatest growth potential for a given level of additional investment?

Wholesaler-distributors with above average profitability for a supplier and superior growth prospects represent the best future channel partners. Encourage your suppliers to recognize your company's contribution, especially if your company is not the largest wholesaler-distributor in the market. If your company falls into this group, consider what additional services or support a supplier could provide. For example, a dedicated account manager from a supplier could provide access to growth programs, customized product development resources, and innovative online promotional programs.

Wholesale distribution executives should take a critical look at internal processes and policies to determine whether their companies are effective partners. Distributors will risk losing product authorization if their distribution costs are too high, their companies are growing too slowly, or their companies lack marketplace clout.

2. Master the financial dynamics of a services business.

Fee-based services require service-oriented metrics such as personnel utilization rates and the profitability of alternative service lines. Traditional reseller-oriented metrics such as inventory turns and sales per employee do not provide adequate insights into the profit dynamics of a services business.

We interviewed and consulted with wholesaler-distributors that have developed a simple markup approach based on average hourly wages. For example, one wholesaler-distributor adds a 30% gross margin to an employee's hourly wage rate to compute an hourly billing rate charge for services. However, this approach is absolutely incorrect when managing a services organization as the following example demonstrates.

A midsized industrial automation controls distributor has a staff of highly knowledgeable application engineers who provide presales technical support to salespeople, postsales training for customers, and other custom work. The overall services business was unprofitable and a standard income statement analysis did not offer any specific clues.

In fact, the key missing metric for this distributor was the *utilization rate*—the percentage of an engineer's total available hours that were actually billed to a customer. Theoretically, there are a maximum of 1,900 working hours in a year, assuming an 8-hour workday and subtracting vacation, holiday, and sick time.

Application engineers spent their available work time on a mix of activities that could be billed to clients and nonbillable activities such as administration, professional development, and selling additional project work. Our review of timesheets discovered that actual utilization rates were about 20%. In other words, application engineers were only able to generate fees for 1 of 5 days each week.

Further analysis revealed that sales reps would frequently quote customers a fixed rate for a services project without knowing how many hours a project would actually require. As a result, many customers were not charged for all of the hours that the wholesaler-distributor's employees actually worked on a project and this reduced effective utilization rates.

Exhibit 3-8 demonstrates the relationship between utilization rate and break-even hourly billing rate for three different wage rates and varying utilization rates. The 100% utilization rate, while clearly not realistic, provides a useful benchmark on the marginal profitability of a services employee. Billing rates would have to be nearly $300 per hour for the distributor to break even with only 20% utilization. That rate was far above competitive engineering services.

Applying these new metrics allowed this wholesaler-distributor to restructure its services business with the following activities:

- Sales reps were provided with management-developed price ranges for 22 common engineering services. The ranges were based on actual time on similar projects.

- Product pricing was increased whenever engineering services were bundled with the product cost.

- The distributor always showed the customer a total services invoice (at standard hourly rates), even when the customer was not charged. This allowed the company to clearly document the value of time spent on engineering services to its customers.

- Hourly billing rates were benchmarked against nonwholesale distribution engineering firms that provided similar services.

The outcome was a substantial increase in company profitability.

3. Avoid overconfidence in the unique value of wholesale distribution logistics.

The growth of fee-for-service logistics can be a double-edged sword for the wholesale distribution channel. The same factors that enable wholesaler-distributors to unbundle their services also provide an opening for logistics companies. It is dangerous to overestimate the uniqueness of the wholesale distribution channel's services.

Consider the channel strategy of **Imperial Tobacco Canada** (ITC, www.ImperialTobaccoCanada.com), the Canadian subsidiary of British American Tobacco (BAT) and one of the largest tobacco companies in Canada. ITC announced plans in Summer 2006 to begin shipping its products to retailers through direct-store delivery, thus effectively eliminating the traditional wholesaler-distributor's role in the channel.

Exhibit 3-8. Example of the relationship between utilization rate and break-even hourly billing rate for a services business.

	Employee A	Employee B	Employee C
Base salary	$30,000	$45,000	$60,000
Implied hourly wage	*$15.79*	*$23.68*	*$31.58*
Benefits and employer-paid taxes	$9,000	$13,500	$18,000
Allocation of overhead	$25,000	$25,000	$25,000
Total Direct Employee Cost	**$64,000**	**$83,500**	**$103,000**

Utilization Rate	Available Hours	Break-even	Billing Rate	Per Hour
100%	1,900	$34	$44	$54
60%	1,140	$56	$73	$90
20%	380	$168	$220	$271

Approximately one-third of tobacco products in Canada are sold through large retailers, but the remainder is sold through small convenience stores. In theory, this fragmentation should preserve a role for wholesaler-distributors. Instead, **Ryder System, Inc.** (www.ryder.com), a transportation and logistics company, will replace wholesale distribution of ITC's products with a delivery system using 200 customized delivery vans and 21 warehouse/cross dock facilities.

Ryder will provide direct-to-store delivery on a fee-for-service basis to more than 26,000 retail locations throughout Canada. In addition, Ryder will design and operate a customized information technology system to provide order visibility and inventory management to retail customers. **The National Convenience Store Distributors Association** (www.nacda.ca), an NAW-member association representing convenience store wholesaler-distributors, expects the Canadian distribution industry to lose thousands of jobs and many wholesalers not to survive. This situation illustrates the dangers of overconfidence when considering providers of logistics services beyond wholesale distribution.

QUESTIONS FOR MANAGEMENT DISCUSSION

Here are discussion questions for your management team. Please review the detailed results for your specific customers and markets in Chapters Six through Eight before discussing these topics.

1. Review the eight possible sources of gross margin for a wholesaler-distributor shown in Exhibit 3-2. What is the relative importance of these profit sources to our company today? Which ones have become more or less important over the past 5 years? How has that affected our business? What do we expect will happen in the next 5 years? What, if anything, have we done to prepare for these changes?

2. Which of our suppliers are most likely to propose or implement a functional discount or fee-for-service compensation approach? What competitive or customer-related factors would lead them to create such a program? Would we benefit or suffer if such a program was implemented by one of our key suppliers?

3. In which of the following areas could third-party logistics companies be a competitive threat to our business?

   - Warehousing
   - Order entry and order processing
   - Order fulfillment to customers
   - Kitting, assembly, or packaging
   - Postsales service or support

   What specific barriers will prevent logistics companies from competing with us?

4. In which areas do we have a sustainable advantage in logistics because of our specialized industry knowledge? How could we develop a fee-based logistics offering using our current distribution infrastructure?

5. List the three most important business problems facing our 10 largest customers. What services could we provide that would solve these problems for our customers? What are the cost elements to deliver these services? What quantifiable financial gains can we deliver to our customers? Would our customers be willing to pay a fee separate from product price for any of our company's services? Why or why not?

6. What has been the most successful fee-based service offered to customers by a wholesaler-distributor (our company or a competitor) in our line of trade? Why has this service been so successful? What lessons can we learn about developing future fee-based services for our customers?

CHAPTER FOUR

Connected Customers

SUMMARY

Wholesaler-distributors must fully embrace the Internet in their business operations now that it is a normal part of everyday life in the United States. Since online searching will be a primary way for customers to find new suppliers, wholesaler-distributors should shift their marketing resources online to reach potential customers in the places that customers might look for a supplier. Online collaboration tools such as online work spaces and virtual trade shows will emerge as new ways for wholesaler-distributors to interact with their customers. However, customers will increasingly gather information from other customers, allowing them to bypass traditional marketing messages from both upstream manufacturers and their wholesaler-distributors.

Adoption of self-service technologies, which has grown significantly in the past 3 years, will continue, so wholesaler-distributors must allow customers to gain information, place an order, or solve simple problems themselves when appropriate. Success in the ever-evolving online business environment will require wholesaler-distributors to use their Web sites as an effective sales lead generation tool to respond to their customers' expectations for online information and to teach their sales reps to sell and communicate using new online technologies.

Data Points
- In 2006, 147 million American adults were Internet users. Approximately 84 million of these users had high-speed Internet connection at home.
- Approximately 23% of wholesaler-distributors have had customers ask their companies to match prices customers gathered from the Internet.
- About 65% of wholesaler-distributors expect to use Web advertising by 2012.

BUSINESS WILL USE THE INTERNET
IN THE SAME WAYS CONSUMERS DO

Research by the Pew Internet and American Life Project (www.pewinternet.org), a nonprofit research initiative that has been surveying large samples of Americans throughout the past 7 years, shows the Internet quickly becoming a normal part of everyday life in the United States.[18] Our research demonstrates that these changes in American society will rapidly spill over to business customers' interactions with wholesaler-distributors. Therefore, it is worthwhile to understand the following facts about today's Internet reality in the broader U.S. population:

- **Internet penetration continues to reach new highs.** In 2006, 147 million American adults were Internet users. About 84 million of these users had high-speed Internet connection at home. The Internet crosses all generational lines, with one-third of those age 65 and older regularly using the Internet. No distributor can reasonably argue that "my customers are different" anymore!

- **Internet use is increasingly unlinked from a deskbound computer.** Some 30% of online Americans access the Internet wirelessly using cell phones and other mobile devices. According to a study cited by Pew, the average American spends more time communicating and using media devices—television, radio, e-mail, cell phones, iPods—than any other activity while awake.

- **People use the Internet for more purposes as they gain more experience online.** Internet experience leads people to perform a greater variety of online activities, use the Internet for work-related applications (such as interacting with a wholesaler-distributor), engage in more significant e-mail exchanges, and perform more financial transactions.

Most significantly for wholesaler-distributors, the Internet is used primarily for information and communication and less for purchasing products. According to Pew surveys of daily Internet usage, "buying a product" occurs much less frequently than activities such as sending e-mail, using a search engine, getting news, researching a hobby, or doing research for school or work.

Research by the Pew Internet and American Life Project identifies some ways in which the Internet is already changing media usage and social interactions:[19]

- **The media universe is fracturing into many more niches.** Traditional information sources such as TV news and newspapers are much less important. An increasing number of people prefer to use the Internet to get news and information. For example, personal news feeds or customized news Web sites are replacing "expert news judgment" about what is important and relevant.

- **Expectations about the availability of people and data keep growing.** People expect others to be accessible via e-mail. They also expect to go online and find communities they want to join. Internet users have the tools and the desire to share and consume word-of-mouth information from other Internet users.

The Internet is also emerging as a key decision-making tool because it connects us and allows us to draw on a broad social network of people for advice or to share experiences. A major Pew study of Internet use found that advice, support, and expert services are primary uses for the Internet about important life decisions, such as choosing a school for a child, making a major investment, or helping someone deal with a major illness.

This social network effect is even more profound when we consider that 48 million adult Internet users have posted some sort of content on the Internet. This user-generated content ranges from photos, stories, and product reviews to Web pages and online journals. About 36% of those over age 30 have been online content creators, and this is further evidence that the current Internet phenomenon crosses generational boundaries.

MANY (BUT NOT ALL) CUSTOMER INTERACTIONS WILL MIGRATE ONLINE

An increasing number of customers will be interacting with their wholesaler-distributors online. The key will be to make it easy for customers to work with wholesaler-distributors in whatever ways they choose.

Our 2004 report highlighted how the Internet is enabling new modes of online self-service and self-management. The most common activities for which customers are taking more responsibility include:

- Gathering product information and specifications from a Web site
- Obtaining product prices and availability information online
- Reviewing purchasing history online
- Accessing postsales technical support information online.

Our research continues to show that online activities will not necessarily overtake other methods of interacting with customers, however. Customers will gravitate toward self-service when they can perform activities that bring them added value (such as becoming better informed about product options online regardless of a wholesaler-distributor's line card) or simply save them time (such as checking order status online instead of placing a call). The Action Ideas section at the end of this chapter describes how a distributor can develop a self-service strategy that balances costs incurred, costs avoided, revenues, and quality of the customer experience.

Adoption of these self-service technologies, which has grown significantly in the past 3 years, will continue. For example, the percentage of customers gathering price information from a wholesaler-distributor's Web site has more than doubled since 2003 and is expected to more than double again by 2012. By then, a wholesaler-distributor without a Web presence will not even exist for prospects searching on the Internet.

Different industries and customer types will adopt these tools faster than others. Only 3% of contractors reviewed their purchasing history online in 2006, while 12% of retail stores and dealers performed this self-service activity. The percentages will increase to 29% and 44% respectively by 2012.

Online ordering will continue to grow as a percentage of wholesaler-distributors' sales revenues through 2012. (See Exhibit 4-1.) The averages by market range from 11% (building materials and contractor supplies) to 31% (finished retail goods). More detailed findings are presented in Part Two of this report. Online ordering includes:

- E-mails sent by a customer to a wholesaler-distributor
- Online ordering via a distributor's Web site
- Online ordering via a third-party Web site
- Orders sent via an EDI connection.

The greatest growth in online buying will come from orders entered online via a wholesaler-distributor's Web site. As in our previous studies, we found that more than 90% of wholesaler-distributors of all sizes expect to have an Internet storefront for online ordering. The pace of change will vary significantly depending on the market, so be sure to review the material in Chapters Six through Eight to understand the specific results for wholesaler-distributors in different markets.

Nevertheless, online buying will not replace traditional ordering approaches (such as the telephone, fax, or in-person and counter sales), which is consistent with the broader Internet developments highlighted earlier in this chapter. The growth rates are consistent with forecasts for online ordering by customers presented in both the 2001 and 2004 *Facing the Forces of Change* reports. One executive at a packaging materials distributor commented: "Our Internet sites are generating our fastest

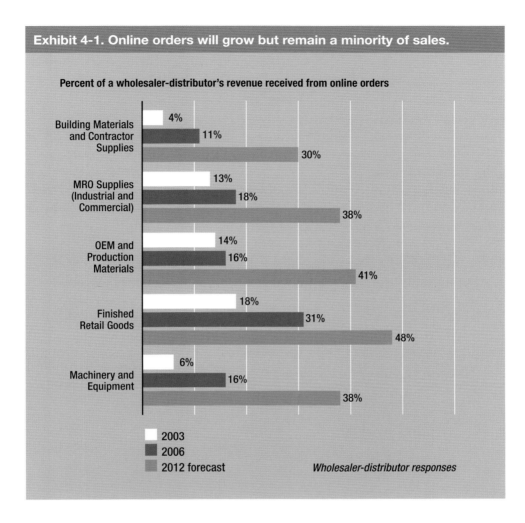

Exhibit 4-1. Online orders will grow but remain a minority of sales.

Percent of a wholesaler-distributor's revenue received from online orders

Building Materials and Contractor Supplies
- 2003: 4%
- 2006: 11%
- 2012 forecast: 30%

MRO Supplies (Industrial and Commercial)
- 2003: 13%
- 2006: 18%
- 2012 forecast: 38%

OEM and Production Materials
- 2003: 14%
- 2006: 16%
- 2012 forecast: 41%

Finished Retail Goods
- 2003: 18%
- 2006: 31%
- 2012 forecast: 48%

Machinery and Equipment
- 2003: 6%
- 2006: 16%
- 2012 forecast: 38%

2003
2006
2012 forecast   *Wholesaler-distributor responses*

growth from all sizes of companies, small to large. But it's still a people-to-people business and I am not sure how much this will go away. We must get more bang for the buck from an outside salesperson to make it worth his time and ours to manage the orders."

The relatively slow adoption of online ordering contrasts sharply with the increasing expectations of the frequency, ease, and method of communication with a wholesaler-distributor's salesforce. Our research uncovered some clear trends:

- E-mail is being adopted in the sales process even faster than predicted in the 2004 report. In 2006, one-third of customers communicated with a wholesaler-distributor's salesforce via e-mail, with limited variation among the different wholesale distribution categories.

- The use of wireless e-mail solutions will jump dramatically because desktop e-mail is poorly suited for mobile employees such as salespeople. Although adoption rates vary by company size, 40% of wholesaler-distributors with revenues below $20 million already have wireless e-mail devices for their salespeople. (See Exhibit 4-2.)

- Wholesale distribution executives should expect to provide corporate e-mail accounts for employees who deal with customers or suppliers. Electronic connectivity will soon become essential given ever-increasing expectations about e-mail accessibility.

Online collaboration tools will also influence the way wholesaler-distributors interact with their customers. Here are five of the most promising technologies with application to wholesale distribution:

- **Instant messaging** (IM) allows direct contact with other Internet users, while simultaneously signaling whether other users are online regardless of their location. For example, customers using IM will expect real-time responses from a sales rep who is online.

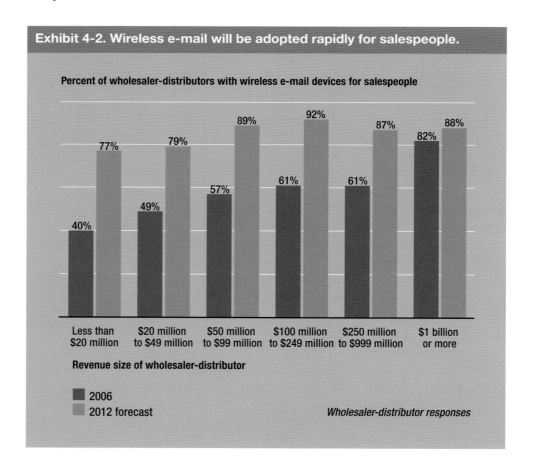

Exhibit 4-2. Wireless e-mail will be adopted rapidly for salespeople.

Percent of wholesaler-distributors with wireless e-mail devices for salespeople

Revenue size of wholesaler-distributor

■ 2006
■ 2012 forecast

Wholesaler-distributor responses

- **Online work spaces** will allow teams from multiple companies to share documents, calendars, databases, and other information in a secure, shared Internet location. These collaboration tools are used regularly in the construction industry to monitor projects for which architects, builders, engineers, general contractors, and distributors all need access to a constantly shifting set of design specifications. These online collaboration tools replace faxes and couriered documents.

- **Live chats** refer to instant messaging applications designed specifically to provide online text assistance to users of a Web site. Our survey research found that wholesale distribution executives expect approximately one-fifth of their customers to engage in a real-time online text chat with an employee by 2012. Surprisingly, this forecast is consistent for wholesaler-distributors of all sizes and in all markets.

- **Click-to-call** technologies allow a customer, by clicking on an icon in an e-mail message or on a Web site, to request a call back at a specific time or talk directly to someone using a microphone attached to his/her computer. Consumer marketers are using these technologies and report much higher response rates than simply listing an 800 number on a Web site. Like live chats, this technology will benefit wholesaler-distributors with online storefronts because they can intercept and answer customer questions in real time.

- **Online trade shows.** This emerging technology platform allows a wholesaler-distributor to host a sales event on the Internet that mimics the experience of an in-person trade show. Attendees at the show see an exhibit floor with vendor booths. Once inside a booth, customers have options similar to a real trade show, such as getting product information or purchasing at a special deal price. They can also initiate an online chat or telephone conversation with vendor representatives.

Although not widely known, online trade shows are starting to be used by wholesaler-distributors serving retailer and dealer customers who may not typically travel to an in-person event. **Five Star Distributors** (www.fivestardist.com), a privately held distributor in the vending product industry, now gets 12% of its annual sales revenue by hosting biannual online selling events at a proprietary Web site (www.virtualvendshow.com). Other distributors that report success with virtual trade shows include grocery wholesaler **C&S Wholesale Grocers** (www.cswg.com) and hardware hardlines distributor **Emery-Waterhouse Company** (www.emeryonline.com).

WHOLESALER-DISTRIBUTORS' MARKETING BUDGETS WILL MOVE ONLINE

The online advertising market is booming along with high rates of Internet penetration. According to the Interactive Advertising Bureau (www.iab.net), total Internet advertising revenues were $12.5 billion in 2005, more than double 2003's revenues of $6.0 billion. Revenues in the third quarter of 2006 were 33% above the same period in 2005. The Internet now accounts for approximately 5% of total U.S. advertising spending and continues to gain market share.

Online searching will be a primary way for customers to find new suppliers. The largest segment of online ad revenues is forecasted to be online search advertising, a system in which advertisers pay online companies to list and/or link their companies' domain names to specific search words and phrases. Typically, the advertiser only pays when a user clicks on the link.

While consumer advertisers represent the largest category of current Internet advertising, the Internet will also be a critical tool for buyers and sellers in business-to-business markets. For example, a ThomasNet.com survey of 590 industrial buyers found that 54% of these buyers used the Internet as their first step when sourcing products and services, compared to only 19% who started with known suppliers.[20] These buyers spent an average of 8 hours per week searching online.

Many wholesaler-distributors already use paid search advertising as evidenced by the number of wholesale distribution companies that appear when either general search terms such as *industrial supplies* or specific products lines are entered into major search sites. Our research found the following clear evidence that almost all wholesaler-distributors will shift marketing resources online to reach potential customers in the places that customers might look for a wholesale distribution supplier:

- **A majority of wholesaler-distributors will use the Internet as a tool to acquire new customers.** Nearly 80% of wholesaler-distributors currently use their company's Web site as a way to generate sales leads. (See Exhibit 4-3.) Looking forward, the proportion of wholesaler-distributors using e-mail marketing will jump from 31% in 2006 to 82% of companies by 2012. About 65% of wholesaler-distributors expect to use Web advertising by 2012, although few see Web advertising as the most important method.

- **The Internet will become a critical method of customer acquisition for many wholesaler-distributors.** In-person sales calls will remain the most important method for generating new sales leads, although corporate Web sites and e-mail marketing will become more important. (See Exhibit 4-4.) About 34%

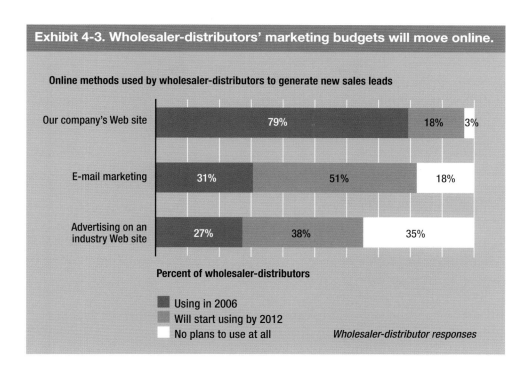

Exhibit 4-3. Wholesaler-distributors' marketing budgets will move online.

Online methods used by wholesaler-distributors to generate new sales leads

Method	Using in 2006	Will start using by 2012	No plans to use at all
Our company's Web site	79%	18%	3%
E-mail marketing	31%	51%	18%
Advertising on an industry Web site	27%	38%	35%

Percent of wholesaler-distributors

■ Using in 2006
■ Will start using by 2012
□ No plans to use at all

Wholesaler-distributor responses

Exhibit 4-4. The Internet will become a critical tool for generating new sales leads.

Most Important Method for Generating New Sales Leads	2006	2012 Forecast	Change
In-person sales call	80%	55%	-25%
Telemarketing	7%	8%	+1%
In-person event or seminar	3%	5%	+2%
Trade show	2%	1%	-1%
Direct mail solicitation	2%	2%	—
Our company's Web site	2%	17%	+15%
E-mail marketing	1%	10%	+9%
All other methods	3%	2%	-1%

Percent of wholesaler-distributors that rate method as "most important"

Wholesaler-distributor responses

of wholesaler-distributors with revenues below $20 million rated their corporate Web site or e-mail marketing as the most important method by 2012, but only 8% of wholesaler-distributors with revenues above $1 billion rated these methods as most important. This dichotomy reflects the opportunity perceived by smaller companies to be identified as a new supplier, whereas larger companies are already well known.

Modern Group Ltd. (www.moderngroup.com), an employee-owned distributor of materials handling and construction equipment in the Mid-Atlantic region, demonstrates many leading-edge practices through its use of the Internet for marketing including the following:

- The company pays a search engine optimization consultant to scan for the best keywords to drive Web site traffic. As a result, they currently get more than 8,000 unique visitors each month.

- Unsolicited inbound e-mails have become one of the most important sources of new customer leads. To encourage even more e-mail inquiries, the company's Web site features the name and personal e-mail address of all senior executives, including the CEO.

- Modern Group advertises used equipment through the largest third-party online industry database in its industry. Web site visitors who access this database from the Modern Group home page will be sent to a customized storefront built from the database listings. The company also operates its own storefront on eBay.

- The company pays for prequalified online quote requests from a third-party online marketplace that matches buyers with up to five potential sellers. This marketplace generates more than 200 new leads per month.

Over time, salespeople have learned that e-mail leads are equal to or better than leads generated through traditional means. Nevertheless, all inbound e-mails and quote requests are screened and routed by the vice president of marketing who ensures that every e-mail gets a response from either an inside or outside salesperson within 8 hours.

CUSTOMERS WILL GET INDEPENDENT
PRICING INFORMATION ONLINE

Another implication of current technology trends is that customers will do more presales information-gathering activities, often at the expense of interacting with a wholesaler-distributor's salespeople. Many wholesaler-distributors will feel the negative implications of this increase in online activity.

Almost one-quarter of wholesaler-distributors are already confronting an uncomfortable scenario: A customer searches online for the best deal on a top-selling product, prints out the Web page showing how much it will cost with shipping, and then asks his/her wholesaler-distributor to match that price. By 2012, nearly 70% of wholesale distribution executives expect customers to ask them to match prices that their customers gathered from the Internet. (See Exhibit 4-5.)

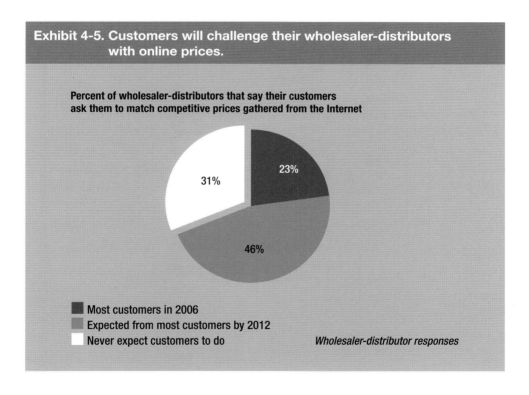

Exhibit 4-5. Customers will challenge their wholesaler-distributors with online prices.

Percent of wholesaler-distributors that say their customers ask them to match competitive prices gathered from the Internet

- 23%
- 46%
- 31%

- ■ Most customers in 2006
- ■ Expected from most customers by 2012
- □ Never expect customers to do

Wholesaler-distributor responses

The strategies of two large Internet companies provide leading insight into the future availability of information:

- **eBay.** Although a leader in the online marketplace, eBay is best known for its consumer auctions. Its Business and Industrial category (www.ebaybusiness.com) now sells more than $1.5 billion of merchandise annually. The Industrial MRO category lists more than 100,000 items. Sellers include wholesaler-distributors looking for new accounts, customers with dead stock or excess inventory, and various online-only storefronts.

- **Froogle™.** Google now offers a free online search engine for locating and comparing prices through its Froogle service (www.froogle.google.com/). Unlike eBay, Froogle does not actually sell any products or promote particular sellers. Froogle gathers its listings in two ways. First, it uses product information submitted electronically by sellers. Second, it automatically includes products listed for sale on Web pages identified by Google's automated software scans of the Internet. In other words, product listings will appear in Froogle whether a seller takes action or does nothing. Froogle also offers price comparisons via text messaging, so even a contractor with a cell phone can do a price check from the field.

Wholesale distribution executives should expect that customers will regularly combine online information with traditional offline channels. A customer will research and interact online, but then place a call to his/her wholesale distribution sales rep or visit a branch to make a purchase. Wholesaler-distributors will also feel price pressure from Internet-savvy customers. An executive for a food distributor noted: "More and more of our customers have either PCs or laptops with high-speed Internet access. I expect more information to be flowing through the Internet."

CUSTOMERS WILL COLLABORATE VIA ONLINE FORUMS

Internet adoption rates suggest that customers will increasingly gather information from other customers, allowing them to bypass traditional marketing messages from both upstream manufacturers and their wholesaler-distributors. The most popular way for people with similar interests to connect online is via Internet forums.[21] There are several hundred thousand active online forums in the United States today. Online users make an estimated 1.3 million posts per day. Internet forums are also commonly referred to as *Web forums, message boards, discussion boards, discussion forums, discussion groups, bulletin boards*, and simply *forums*.

Forums bring together people with similar interests across time and geography. The format is very simple. Someone posts a message that is visible to everyone. You read it and then have the option to post a reply that will also be visible to everyone. Discussions can build up without all users having to be online at the same time. An archive of discussions and questions is available for search. Purely commercial messages are excluded from forum postings, either by a moderator or by the negative reaction from the community.

These groups have powerful network effects: The online forum becomes more and more valuable as the number of participants increases. The growth in Internet activity is now creating highly specialized forums of customers of wholesaler-distributors. Exhibit 4-6 lists a representative sample of 21 active forums with participants who would be customers of wholesaler-distributors. Typical topics of conversations in these forums include:

- Product advice and experiences
- Buying experiences with different vendors
- Recommendations for sourcing products
- Maintenance and repair details
- General business management.

These online forums will present another challenge to the perceived value of wholesaler-distributors. Customers will increasingly be able to use the Internet to answer questions, resolve problems, and get advice from other customers. These communities will provide an alternative to interactions with wholesale distribution sales or customer service personnel.

Consider **Contractor Talk**™ (www.contractortalk.com), which bills itself as the "Professional Construction and Remodeling Forum—Where the Trades Meet!" The site is emerging as one of the most active communities for professional trade contractors. As of July 2006, there were 7,800 registered members and more than 113,000 messages posted on 26 different message boards.

Today, the most active groups are forming among smaller customers who traditionally are the most dependent on wholesale distribution inside or outside salespeople to obtain technical and business assistance in product selection and use. Wholesaler-distributors no longer have a lock on information needed by these customers to make purchasing and sourcing decisions, since other customers will make more and more information available online. Forums also provide much richer and more meaningful information than typical static information available online such as product specifications, material safety data sheets, and brochures.

As with many trends discussed in this report, the growth of online forums can also provide advantages for wholesaler-distributors. In the Action Ideas section at the end of this chapter, we suggest ways that wholesaler-distributors can take advantage of this shift in customer behavior.

Exhibit 4-6. Examples of online forums where distribution customers connect.

Web Site	Products/Markets
BUILDING MATERIALS AND CONTRACTOR SUPPLIES	
www.contractortalk.com	Professional Trade Contractors (all products)
www.glassfiles.com	Architectural and Automotive glass
www.jlconline.com	Drywall, Ceramic Tile, Framing, Doors and Windows
www.lawnsite.com	Lawn Care and Landscaping
www.stonepowerhouse.com	Natural Stone
www.turnwood.net	Woodworking and Cabinetry
www.wef.org	Wastewater Treatment and Water Quality Protection
www.woodweb.com	Cabinets and Millwork
MRO SUPPLIES	
www.cleaning.com	Janitorial and Cleaning Products
www.dentaltown.com	Dentists
www.firehouse.com	Firefighters and Emergency Responders
www.fmanet.org	Metal Forming, Fabricating, and Welding
www.fmforum.org	Facilities Managers
www.maintenanceforums.com	Plant Machinery Maintenance
www.ntma.org	Tooling and Machining
RETAIL STORES AND DEALERS	
http://groups.msn.com/ TheRestaurantManagersForum	Bar and Restaurant Managers
www.retailindustry.about.com	Consumer Products (Retail Management)
www.furnitureresource.info	Contract Furniture and Interior Design
MACHINERY AND EQUIPMENT	
www.eturbines.com	Power Generation Equipment
www.heavyequipmentforums.com	Construction Equipment
www.tractorbynet.com	Tractors

Online forums can usually be accessed from the Web site's home page and are labeled "Discussion," "Message Board," or "Forum."

MANUFACTURERS WILL EXPAND DIRECT ONLINE CUSTOMER INTERACTIONS

The Internet also gives manufacturers (suppliers to wholesaler-distributors) an affordable way to bypass traditional distribution or media channels in order to communicate directly with end customers. A survey of industrial manufacturing marketing executives found that more than one-half considered their Web site to be their most powerful marketing tool.[22]

For example, many branded consumer products manufacturers are establishing their own private label online communities, including message boards, around their leading brands as a way to provide content, build brand loyalty, and deepen relationships with end consumers. Prominent examples include **Campbell Soup** (kitchentable-campbells.forums.liveworld.com) and **Coca-Cola** (www.mycoke.com).

While only a handful of business-to-business manufacturers are attempting to build these types of online communities now, more manufacturer-sponsored online forums will spring up as online usage grows. Online communities of product users will be most logical for manufacturers, who for example, want to connect with trade contractors using a particular type of power tool, or with plant maintenance engineers who work with a specific type of capital equipment.

One current example is the Web site run by **Hobart Welders** (www.hobartwelders.com), a manufacturer of industrial quality welders. This site provides standard product and sales information such as material safety data sheets, owner's manuals, and a distributor locator. What is most intriguing is that the site has a very active online forum for its users called **Weld Talk** (www.hobartwelders.com/mboard). There are more than 200,000 archived posts and more than 8,000 registered users, providing Hobart with real-time insight into the applications and problems experienced by its customers. Before the Internet, it was simply not possible for a manufacturer selling through wholesaler-distributors to get this type of unfiltered feedback in a cost-effective way.

The growth in online searching will also shift more power to upstream suppliers, especially for lead generation. Using online searching, a customer will start at the manufacturer's site for new purchases or infrequent buys of complex products, capital expenditures, specification searches, or purchased products. Once the presale selection is made at the manufacturer's site, the buyer links through the Internet directly to the wholesaler-distributor's site, where the actual order is taken. This type of buying process was first described as the Coordinated Channels scenario in our 2001 report *Facing the Forces of Change: Future Scenarios for Wholesale Distribution*.

Our survey of manufacturing executives found that 83% of manufacturer-suppliers in 2006 did not offer to sell directly to end customers. In fact, most appeared to leverage their online presence to generate leads for their distribution channel.

For example, **Swagelok Company** (www.swagelok.com), a privately held manufacturer of fluid system products, provides detailed online product information about its more than 15,000 products for design engineers and purchasing managers. However, Swagelok products are sold exclusively through a network of 240 independently authorized sales and service distributors. Potential customers must register with a local distributor in order to purchase online or to get a price quote, although they can also locate the phone number of an authorized distributor by entering their geographic location.

Manufacturers with broader distribution networks and more authorized wholesaler-distributors will be more likely to hand off a potential buying opportunity. For example, the **Bosch Power Tools** (www.boschtools.com) division of the Bosch Group provides a detailed online product catalog. Each product page links buyers to the online storefronts of four resellers. Wholesaler-distributors on the site include **Airgas, Inc.** (airgas.com), **Fastenal Company** (www.fastenal.com), and many specialty tool distributors. The company regularly rotates the specific resellers listed on each product page. Like Swagelok, the Bosch Power Tools site offers a geographic locator to find a physical branch or retailer.

Nevertheless, a growing number of manufacturers plan to offer customers the option to purchase products directly from their own sites. Our survey uncovered the following online selling strategies by manufacturer-suppliers:

- While only 17% of manufacturer-suppliers currently sell directly to end customers, this figure will more than double to 40% of manufacturer-suppliers by 2012.

- Smaller manufacturers are more likely to bypass wholesaler-distributors. Our interviews revealed that many executives fear losing control of their customers and want an in-house alternative to the traditional wholesale distribution channel. The Internet now provides a cost-effective, direct-selling channel that can complement independent wholesaler-distributors.

Now that we've looked closely at the connected customers trend, let's look at specific strategies within the following Action Ideas to help you better understand the implications of this trend for your company. This chapter closes with Questions for Management Discussion that you and your team can tackle right away.

ACTION IDEAS

1. Use the Internet as an effective lead generation tool.

Customers will increasingly use the Internet as a primary way to gather information and find new suppliers even if the actual purchase is not made online. Therefore, your company's Web site must function as an effective sales lead generation tool, not just as an online e-commerce platform. Senior wholesale distribution executives must make sure that their sites deliver a compelling message about their company, allow prospects to take action, and connect online prospects with appropriate sales resources. Here are some best practices recommended by Web marketing experts and adapted to wholesale distribution:

- **Be visible online.** Make sure that your company's Web site can be found by search engines by including tags that correspond to key words in search engines. Wholesaler-distributors should also devote a portion of their marketing funds to search advertising and hire a company that specializes in optimizing Web sites for online searches.

- **Directly connect Web visitors to your sales team.** You do not want a new customer prospect to abandon your site because he/she can't figure out how to contact you or because he/she has a simple question but doesn't know how to go about asking it. At a basic level, every Web page on your site should have telephone and e-mail contact information. Wholesaler-distributors should also include the names and e-mail addresses for inside and outside salespeople, along with live Click-to-Call or Instant Messaging links. Many people will not even bother sending e-mails to generic mailboxes such as *info@distributor.com*.

- **Humanize the online experience.** Wholesaler-distributors can go one step further by reaching out to Web site visitors. Instead of waiting for a visitor to make a call or send an e-mail, a customer service agent can detect the visitor's presence on a Web site and initiate a real-time conversation. This proactive approach plays to the sales strengths of wholesaler-distributors who are often selling complex items that are rarely suitable for point-and-click purchasing. Office furniture dealer **247 Workspace** (www.247workspace.com) found that potential customers were getting confused by the many choices and information available online. According to the company's CEO, the probability of a sale goes up dramatically once people engage in a text chat with a live person.[23]

- **Be sophisticated about e-mail marketing.** Badly designed or poorly targeted e-mails may actually hurt your sales efforts more than help them. For example, sending the same general e-mail repeatedly to a broad list is unlikely to generate much response and may even get you labeled a *spammer*. Treat investments in e-mail marketing just as seriously as you would investments in a trade show or magazine ad. There are many resources and books available on appropriate e-mail marketing. Read case studies on best practices used by companies such as **Hewlett-Packard** (www.hp.com) whose "Technology at Work" e-mail program was cited by Forrester Research for its effectiveness at driving revenues and boosting customer retention.[24]

- **Track customer behavior for early warning signals.** The online trends described in this chapter will affect different lines of trade at different speeds. Ask inside and outside sales reps to record every situation in which a customer mentions a price quote from a Web search. Store the information in a central database so you can see how quickly your customers are adapting to the world of more transparent prices.

Wholesaler-distributors can also respond to customers' expectations for online information by providing more than just a standard product catalog. Consider **Budnick Converting, Inc.** (www.budnickconverting.com), a privately held, second-generation distributor and converter of adhesive coated tapes and foams. In December 2004, the company launched **Tape Info**™ (www.tapeinfo.com), an adhesive tape search engine that provides information to engineers, purchasing agents, and industrial operations personnel about more than 7,000 major brand tapes. TapeInfo.com, which is rated as one of the top 10 best business-to-business Web sites by *BtoB magazine*, takes advantage of customers' Internet usage by serving as both lead generation and online purchasing site. Prior to the site's launch, Budnick received only phone orders. In 2006, Budnick received 25% of its orders online and got one-half of its new sales leads from the site, even though the products described on TapeInfo.com are available from many other sellers.

2. Prepare your salesforce for the online future.

The availability of online information does not mean that customers will stop buying from wholesaler-distributors and it does not signal the end of the salesforce. Consider these comments from an executive at a paper, packaging, and janitorial supplies distribution company: "E-commerce will be much more pervasive for our customers and suppliers, and therefore, our own business processes. The outside sales professionals' role will not go away, but these salespeople will need to provide more value for our customers and our company."

Here are some of the competencies that sales managers should consider for their sales team (and themselves):

- **Teach salespeople how to write e-mails.** E-mail is moving from a personal communication medium to a business tool, making proper usage essential. This type of training should range from basic competencies, such as proper grammar and spelling, to more subtle skills, such as appropriate e-mail etiquette and how to convey complex ideas in words.

- **Make sure salespeople take the Internet seriously.** The successful wholesaler-distributors interviewed for this study all mentioned difficulties in getting sales-people to take e-mail leads as seriously as phone calls. Many salespeople will stick with the most familiar technology, usually the telephone. Since e-mail users often expect a very rapid response, they can judge a wholesaler-distributor via e-mail communication prior to spending time with the distributor on the phone. Set up policies for screening and routing all inbound e-mails and quote requests.

- **Provide technology training to your salesforce.** Be sure each salesperson is comfortable selling through new technologies and can teach customers how to gain information, place an order, and solve simple problems themselves. For example, a sales rep should be able to teach customers how to access your company's Web site for product information, special marketing promotions, and account information.

- **Train your inside and outside salesforce on how to respond consistently and appropriately when customers present prices found on the Internet.** Inside and outside salespeople should be able to explain clearly and concisely the specific services that make your wholesale distribution company a valuable supplier of services, instead of merely a provider of readily available goods. Distribution sales executives should evaluate each of their salespeople to determine if he or she needs training in qualifying customers, uncovering problems, identifying solutions, and bringing the company's resources together for problem solving.

- **Re-evaluate policies for authorizing competitive price matching.** Our inter-views revealed that many wholesaler-distributors in 2006 would never match online prices, choosing instead to redirect the conversation to the value of their companies' services. Other distributors have no consistent policies for dealing with online prices, even though our research found that one-quarter of wholesaler-distributors are already dealing with these customer interactions.

The online world is developing quickly. Senior wholesale distribution executives should designate one person in their company to follow new developments such as the availability of online price information and the emergence of new customer online forums. Make sure that any new insights are communicated to the key business decision makers on a regular basis.

3. Design a customer-focused self-service strategy.

As the Internet moves into the mainstream, a wholesaler-distributor's self-service strategy must balance the trade-offs between costs-to-serve and the quality of the customer experience. Some customers and situations are better off with a people-dominant interaction, while others can best be handled with a technology-dominant interaction. The worst case situation would be to replace a competent sales team with a Web self-service application that confuses customers.

In the 2004 report, we described how self-service can be a cost-effective alternative for customers whose level of spend does not justify labor-intensive interactions. However, the goal should never be to indiscriminately push customer relationships to your company's Web site if that compromises the customer's service experience. It is clearly self-defeating to lower a valuable customer's likelihood of ever purchasing from your company again simply in the hope of getting a short-term cost reduction.

Exhibit 4-7 provides a framework to help distribution executives evaluate their self-service investments and strategy. There are two primary questions to consider:

- **How valuable is this customer?** According to our survey, 7 out of 10 distributors currently measure the profitability of individual customers. Most executives recognize that total sales dollars with an account are insufficient to understand true customer profitability. There is no reason to treat all customers the same when it comes to self-service.

- **How important is a conversation with a real person?** The interface must be matched to the appropriate task. Online-savvy customers can easily review their purchasing history online, but new sales opportunities should be routed to an appropriate salesperson. A sales conversation with a valuable customer is more important than a routine billing inquiry. Online lead conversions are most effective when followed up rapidly by communication from a salesperson.

Evaluate your current self-service strategy against this framework. The trade-offs inherent in Exhibit 4-7 highlight that it is counter productive to push customers into Web self-service simply to spread the fixed costs of technology investments. Instead, self-service technologies should support the broader strategy of retaining and growing your most valuable customers.

If self-service is not effective, customers will expect a logical and consistent pathway to solve a problem or to get help, such as a phone number or e-mail address. Assisted service, such as a live Web chat, is especially useful for online resolution. There must be a linkage between your online presence and your inside sales staff, so that customers do not have to start all over every time they interact with your company.

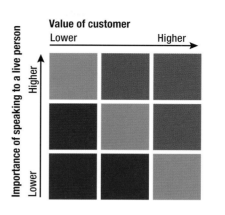

Exhibit 4-7. Building a customer-focused self-service strategy.

■ Assign relationship manager who can manage appropriate use of self-service for supply chain efficiency

■ Focus on automated self-service, but provide easy access to account relationship manager or salesperson

■ Send to automated self-service

Value of customer

Lower — Higher

Importance of speaking to a live person — Higher / Lower

Consider the following disguised example. A privately held distributor was struggling to improve bottom-line profits. This company produced regular financial reports about its three major business segments; however, it did not know anything about the profitability or cost to serve any individual account. After extracting readily available data from the company's information system, management discovered that many active accounts had average gross margins per delivery below the company's break-even delivery expenses. The company was also able to challenge conventional wisdom about large customers by showing that active accounts with higher gross margin dollars were bigger because these large customers ordered more frequently and not because they placed larger orders.

These fact-based insights, drawn from customer-level analytics, led management to ask: "How can we have profitable relationships with the customers that benefit most from working with us?" Management began proactive discussions with the most profitable customers to identify win-win relationship strategies for building loyalty and lowering joint transaction costs. The company also began providing its full suite of value-added services to the most profitable customers only and moved away from a *one-size-fits-all* service model.

In contrast, the bottom 20% of accounts was highly unprofitable and absorbed one-half of the company's total gross margin dollars. Self-service technologies were a win-win alternative because these customers did not provide the gross margin dollars to justify labor-intensive interactions or frequent deliveries.

QUESTIONS FOR MANAGEMENT DISCUSSION

Here are discussion questions for your management team. Please review the detailed results for your specific customers and markets in Chapters Six through Eight before discussing these topics.

1. How do our customers use the Internet in their jobs today, *excluding* interactions with our company? How do they expect to use the Internet in the future?

2. Are our salespeople sufficiently trained in handling and responding to e-mail? Do our salespeople view leads from inbound e-mails to be more or less valuable than leads generated from other sources such as telemarketing or response cards? Are their perceptions accurate? What could we do to make sure that inbound e-mails receive the appropriate follow-up?

3. Imagine that our company is a prospective customer of the products sold by our company. By visiting our company's Web site, how easily can we find the following information?

    • General phone number and physical mailing address
    • E-mail and phone contact information for a specific person in charge of new customer accounts
    • E-mail and phone contact information for the person responsible for handling RFPs and RFQs

    Visit our competitors' Web sites and answer these same questions.

4. Search for possible suppliers of products sold by our company using a well-known, online search tool such as Google.com or Yahoo.com. Try to limit our search to companies operating within our geographic regions. How many potential suppliers can we identify? How are competing suppliers using online advertising? Which of our competitors are paying for search terms?

5. Talk to customers who have used online forums (such as the examples in Exhibit 4-6). What information were they searching for? Did they find what they wanted? How did their experiences compare with contacting a salesperson or customer service agent at our company?

6. Prior to our company's next sales meeting, ask our sales reps to search online for the prices of our company's best-selling products and report back on what they learn. Discuss which of our products are at risk of becoming more commoditized if customers begin shopping for the lowest price bidder.

CHAPTER FIVE Emerging Trends

SUMMARY

This chapter reviews three emerging trends whose ultimate importance and impact is highly uncertain. Over the next few years, these uncertainties will either turn into future forces of change or become unimportant and simply drop off the radar screen. Today, there are credible arguments to support multiple points of view for each trend.

The three emerging trends are

- Acquisition Activity
- The Changing U.S. Workforce
- A Slowdown in Commodity Prices.

ACQUISITION ACTIVITY

The wholesale distribution industry is going through a very active wave of merger and acquisition activity led by both strategic buyers and financial buyers. Following a lull in the early part of the decade, announced acquisitions have more than quadrupled in the past 2 years for wholesaler-distributors in construction, and industrial and commercial markets. (See Exhibit 5-1.) These are the markets discussed in Chapters Six and Seven. Unfortunately, comparable data are not available for wholesaler-distributors in retail consumer markets (Chapter Eight). The influx of outside capital is already having an enormous impact on the growth plans and exit strategies of many business owners.

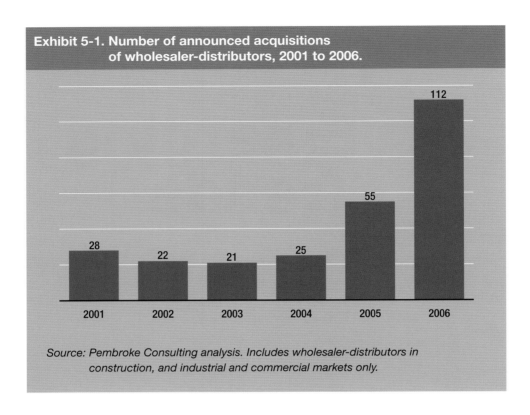

Exhibit 5-1. Number of announced acquisitions of wholesaler-distributors, 2001 to 2006.

Source: Pembroke Consulting analysis. Includes wholesaler-distributors in construction, and industrial and commercial markets only.

Larger public companies are using stock equity and strong balance sheets to purchase private wholesaler-distributors. These strategic buyers seek to expand geographic coverage or add new products or services. In wholesale distribution, acquiring a successful regional company is generally the least expensive way for a buyer to expand operations. Experienced strategic buyers also have a good feel for the true economic value of a target company and postacquisition integration issues. Often, the company is interested in the long-term strategic benefits of an acquisition rather than a short-term payoff.

One of the most active strategic acquirers has been **HD Supply** (www.hdsupplyinc.com), the $12 billion wholesale distribution division of home improvement retailer **The Home Depot** (www.homedepot.com). This division has acquired 33 wholesaler-distributors in the past 10 years, with 24 of those acquisitions occurring in the past 2 years. Two of its largest acquisitions were billion dollar wholesaler-distributors **National Waterworks Holdings** in 2005 and **Hughes Supply** in 2006. The acquisition of Hughes Supply doubled HD

Supply's annual sales. The Home Depot forecasts that HD Supply's revenues will be between $23 billion and $27 billion by 2010, which would represent an estimated 18% to 19% of The Home Depot's total revenues.

Wholesale distribution is also one of the top targets for buyout investments by private equity firms. These financial buyers are displaying a far greater ability and willingness to pay premium prices for leading distribution companies. They are being attracted by the ongoing need for wholesale distribution to end markets insulated from global competition, such as facilities maintenance, construction, or health care services. Some analysts have estimated that private equity firms are currently looking to invest approximately $100 billion of uninvested capital, which represents at least $400 billion in buying power at current leverage multiples.

In contrast to a strategic buyer, a financial buyer purchases a wholesaler-distributor as an investment and therefore looks at the potential return that a company can generate. Financial buyers are effectively buying the cash flow generated by a business, whereas a strategic buyer is purchasing a synergistic, strategic addition to its existing operations. The financial buyer will finance the purchase by borrowing against the assets and future cash flows of the acquired company. It will pay down the debt by increasing operating cash flows through reduction of operating expenses and elimination of surplus assets.

A financial buyer is less likely to make management changes to an acquired company, preferring that the owner and managers of an acquired wholesaler-distributor remain with the new company. In some cases, the financial buyer will remain at arm's length from the daily operations of the company. A financial buyer typically expects to own a company for 5 to 7 years.

There are many well-known examples of private equity firms investing in wholesaler-distributors. **Clayton, Dubilier & Rice, Inc.** (www.cdr-inc.com) has made multiple billion-dollar investments in the **Rexel Group** (www.rexel.com), a distributor of electrical equipment and supplies, and **VWR International** (www.vwr.com), a distributor of scientific supplies. Private equity firms **Kelso & Company** (www.kelso.com) and **MSD Capital, L.P.** (www.msdcapital.com) are funding the acquisition activity of **US Electrical Services** (www.usesi.com).

In many cases, the difference between strategic and financial buyers will blur once a private equity-backed company has acquired multiple wholesaler-distributors. At that point, the new entity may operate more like a strategic buyer, although the ultimate goal remains to deliver a financial return to the owner. For example, Rexel acquired General Electric's wholesale distribution business.

Implications for Wholesaler-Distributors

Although executives in most markets expect continued acquisition activity, there is little consensus about the ultimate impact on the wholesale distribution industry.

Some wholesaler-distributors believe that larger and better capitalized companies will gain an advantage by leveraging the combined purchasing power of multiple acquisitions with suppliers. In essence, the combined volume of a larger wholesaler-distributor enables strategic sourcing against manufacturers similar to the process described in Chapter One.

Another possible outcome could be intense competition for customers based on lower pricing. For example, larger companies could decide to accelerate organic growth by offering lower prices, perhaps by passing along any additional supplier discounts derived from their buying power. Independent wholesaler-distributors could feel the ultimate marketplace impact in the form of lower margins. Commenting on HD Supply, one executive told us: "They are already starting to take some of our business away. They are supplying many things like filters, thermostats, A/C units, humidifiers, etc. I see them getting more and more into the business." (HVAC/R parts and equipment)

On the other hand, smaller wholesaler-distributors believe that larger competitors can be overcome with better performance and innovation by small companies. These companies recognize the opportunity to combine a superior understanding of customers' purchasing priorities, while meeting key suppliers' business requirements. One executive expressed this optimism in the following way: "I think [consolidation] will increase the value of the independent distributor related to servicing the customer and providing value to the vendor. The progressive independent will have a distinct service advantage. We will be more nimble and more reactive to local market conditional changes. It will raise the bar on the independent, however." (electrical products)

Midsized wholesaler-distributors could feel the greatest pressure from these competitive dynamics. They will lack the scale advantages of larger companies with multiple locations, while not being as nimble as the smaller wholesale distribution competitors.

Given these uncertainties, wholesale distribution executives should have a strategic plan for their business that recognizes the reality of heightened acquisition activity, yet maintains a focus on profitable growth. Our research and consulting from the last major consolidation cycle of the 1990s[25] provides insight into the three basic strategic options for independent distributors in today's environment: get big, get focused, or get out. All other strategies are ultimately variations on these three options:

- **Get big.** One option is to become the acquirer and consolidate other wholesaler-distributors. Distribution consolidators have been most successful when targeting opportunities that are unavailable to smaller companies, such as the ability to service larger customers or the financial strength to access public capital markets. Successful distribution consolidators all made substantial investments in building solid IT infrastructures, which allowed for rapid integration of an acquired company's customer records, orders, inventory, warehouse operations, transportation, and finances.

  Unfortunately, few distribution consolidators from the 1990s were able to integrate and operate their acquisitions. Typically, these consolidators overemphasized acquisitions at the expense of building an integrated business with a strong operating vision and the discipline to impose that vision on the entire organization. Many consolidators in the quest for scale through standardization were unable to combine the benefits of a large, well-capitalized, and professionally managed corporation with the service and mindset of a wholesale distribution entrepreneur.

- **Get focused.** Well-run, independent distributors continue to thrive even in consolidating industries due to their great skill in maintaining high levels of customer service and generating customer loyalty. Less than 1% of the country's 270,000 wholesaler-distributors have annual revenues above $100 million.[26]

  Wholesaler-distributors can use the acquisition of a competitor as an opportunity to re-engage with their customers. Years of day-to-day account servicing often blinds executives to emerging threats or challenges. Get external, objective survey data from customers to understand how your company and its services are perceived. Assess your vulnerability to a national competitor that could offer enhanced services with lower product prices.

  A modern, scalable IT system should be an essential element of a distributor's focus strategy. Today's technology allows even small companies to have the best of both worlds: local attention and personal visits combined with the type of online services described in Chapter Four. Almost every wholesaler-distributor can afford sophisticated options that allow customers to place orders and handle routine inquiries themselves.

- **Get out.** The courage to face the future honestly often leads owners to look for a profitable exit strategy. Naturally, the best time to sell a company is when there is no financial pressure to repay creditors or create an instant retirement nest egg. However, acquisition dynamics should play a role in the decision, because industries do not consolidate forever, as evidenced by the sharp slowdown in acquisition activity after the peak in 2000.

  Today appears to be a favorable time to get a premium valuation, given the accelerating level of acquisition activity. The accelerating pace of consolidation, along with the money flowing into the wholesale distribution industry, offers an opportunity for smart sellers who understand their options. Selling early also provides more strategic flexibility, because the best companies have the opportunity to create an auction among potential buyers. To learn more about the acquisition process, see the NAW/DREF publication *The Acquisitive Distributor: 4 Keys to Success When Buying a Wholesale Distribution Business* (available at www.nawpubs.org).

THE CHANGING U.S. WORKFORCE

The U.S. workforce is becoming older and more diverse as the baby boomer generation ages, mirroring broader changes in the U.S. population. These changes, which have been predicted for some time, are likely to affect both the internal operations and external markets of distributors. By way of background, the labor force (or workforce) is equal to the total of all employed and unemployed people. The unemployed are defined to be people without a job who are actively looking for one. Students, retirees, and others not looking for a job are not considered to be part of the labor force. Thus, the total growth in the labor force is a function of growth in the population of eligible workers and individual decisions to participate in the labor force. For example, a retiree who decides to begin looking for a job would increase the size of the labor force.

A major study by the nonprofit research organization RAND Corporation[27] summarized the major characteristics of the future workforce:

- **An aging workforce.** The U.S. workforce is forecast to grow by 14.7 million people from 2004 to 2014. However, 77% of that growth will come from people over the age of 55, while the number of people under 24 years of age will actually decline over the same time period. As a result, more than one out of five U.S. workers will be older than age 55 by 2014.

- **Slower labor force growth.** Between 2000 and 2010, the annual growth in the U.S. labor force is projected to equal the rate of 1.1% in the 1990s. However, the rate is projected to slow to 0.4% in the next decade due to the reduced fertility rates following the baby boom that ended in 1964. The oldest baby boomers, who reached 60 years in 2006, will be retiring over the next two decades, so the number of people leaving the workforce will increase sharply.

- **Shifting workforce composition.** Most of the growth in the U.S. labor force has come from the combination of women's increased labor force participation and a large inflow of immigrants. In 2006, more than 60% of women worked in paid employment compared to only 35% in the mid 1960s. After rising for several decades, the labor force participation rate for women has shown no growth in recent years. In contrast, men's labor force participation rates have been declining, so that 47% of the U.S. workforce is now female.

- **More diversity.** Immigration is also increasing and the racial and ethnic diversity of the workforce continues to grow. Asians and Hispanics are the fastest growing racial and ethnic groups in the population and the workforce. The U.S. Bureau of Labor Statistics projects that people of Hispanic origin will be 16% of the civilian labor force in 2014, compared to only 6.6% in 1984.

Some of these changes have already affected the wholesale distribution industry. For example, the U.S. Bureau of Labor Statistics estimates that almost 14% of people employed in wholesale distribution are Hispanic or Latino, which is roughly the same as the percentage in the total U.S. population. In contrast, the percentage of women in the wholesale distribution workforce is only 29%, compared to the overall U.S. average of 47%. The U.S. average is driven by industries with a much greater percentage of women employed, including health care (79%), education (69%), finance (59%), and retailing (49%).

In addition to the direct effect on wholesale distribution companies, these inevitable demographic shifts will have an indirect effect on wholesale distribution by changing the mix of goods and services in the U.S. economy. For example, older people have very different spending patterns compared to younger people and they spend much more on health care and less on insurance, transportation, and entertainment. Similarly, increasing female labor force participation has coincided with the growth of *outsourced* household services, such as child care, cleaning services, prepared meals, and home improvement projects.

Implications for Wholesaler-Distributors

Demographic changes could have substantial impacts on the wholesale distribution industry. However, there will not be a single point in time when these demographic changes will trigger a particular crisis in the wholesale distribution industry. Instead, the changes are occurring gradually and somewhat predictably. This will allow forward-looking wholesale distribution executives to address these planning steps:

- **Identify the gaps.** Evaluate your company's growth plans and the associated personnel needs. Estimate how many of your most valuable employees will be eligible for retirement within the next 5 years. The number of 35- to 44-year-old workers in the workforce will be declining, so wholesaler-distributors must also prepare to compete more aggressively to attract the next generation of managers to their companies.

- **Have a plan to capture knowledge.** At some wholesaler-distributors, the salesperson is the key point of customer contact and a repository of valuable information about each account. The impending retirement of senior salespeople could put customer relationships at risk. Ensure that these individuals in your company have the opportunity to begin sharing their knowledge in a constructive way. For example, you might consider pairing younger and older salespeople on critical accounts far in advance of any prospective retirements to ensure a smooth hand off and knowledge transfer. Naturally, these plans must also ensure that older workers feel secure in their jobs.

- **Develop flexible options for older workers.** Rather than losing key employees, consider developing formal programs that entice older employees to remain on the job past the traditional retirement age of 65. Common options could include phased retirement plans, job-sharing arrangements, or expanded telecommuting opportunities. However, it may be difficult to convince people to postpone their retirement, since the societal trend is toward earlier retirement.

- **Invest in productivity-enhancing technology.** As we note in the Introduction, productivity growth in the wholesale distribution industry exceeded the overall U.S. business sector due to productivity-enhancing technology investments. Productivity is especially crucial to profitability in wholesale distribution because employee compensation costs—salaries, commissions, and benefits—represent 60% to 70% of total operating expenses. Distributors should increase technology spending as a hedge against the negative effects of demographic changes.

- **Consider the indirect effects.** Step back and consider how broad demographic changes might affect the overall prospects and growth opportunities in your line of trade. For example, the trend toward outsourced household services has changed the foodservice distribution business by increasing the importance of supplying prepared foods. Or perhaps consider the opportunities for supplying customers in the health care services industries, which are projected to grow faster than the overall U.S. economy.

A SLOWDOWN IN COMMODITY PRICES

As we discuss in the Introduction, the U.S. wholesale distribution industry is going through a period of remarkable, top-line revenue growth. Lines of trade as diverse as industrial products, pharmaceuticals, and plumbing/HVAC are all registering double-digit growth. Ironically, this growth surge is now setting the stage for a potential competitive challenge for distributors.[28]

Top-line revenue growth comes from selling more products (increasing volume), achieving higher prices for those products (raising prices), or a fortunate combination of both factors. While the current economic expansion boosts unit volume, wholesale distribution executives must recognize that unusually high commodity price inflation is making revenue growth much easier to achieve. In recent years, prices of certain core commodities have literally skyrocketed. For example:

- Steel mill products increased in price by more than 60% since mid 2003. Although prices began to decline in the second half of 2005, prices remained relatively high by historic standards, due in large part to China's commodity-intensive manufacturing activities. (China's imports of all commodities have risen more than tenfold in the past 15 years.)

- Oil remains $60 per barrel versus $32 per barrel in late 2003, triggering energy-related price increases throughout the supply chain and increasing the prices of derivative products. For example, prices for plastic pipes and fittings are now growing at 20% per year.

- Prices for building materials, such as lumber products, spiked in 2004 and remain above historic levels. Inflation for concrete products remains high as demand continues to exceed supply.

The changing pricing environment is evident in the stage-of-processing category from the Producer Price Index (PPI) that measures intermediate materials, supplies, and components. This portion of the PPI is representative of wholesale distribution because it includes both semi-finished goods (such as steel mill products or lumber) and nondurable items purchased by business firms as inputs for their operations (such as diesel fuel, industrial supplies, or paper boxes). After barely increasing from 1992 to 2002, the intermediate materials, supplies, and components portion of the PPI has jumped by 28% since 2002.

This commodity price effect has increased top-line revenue growth for the wholesale distribution industry. Before adjusting for the inflationary effect of changing product prices, year-to-year quarterly revenue growth averaged 6.1% from 1993 through 2002. Although the gap between adjusted and unadjusted growth fluctuated throughout that period, the wholesale distribution industry still experienced consistently positive real growth averaging 4.5%.

The situation in 2007 is substantially different. Year-to-year quarterly revenue growth averaged a healthy 6.8% from 2002 through mid 2006. However, the average growth rate dropped to only 1.9% after adjusting for inflation. In other words, the wholesale distribution industry has experienced limited real growth in the past 2 years, despite historically comparable top-line revenue growth.

Preliminary data from the fourth quarter of 2006 shows slow growth in the intermediate materials, supplies, and components portion of the PPI. We do not yet know whether this is the end of the commodity price bubble or merely a temporary pause.

Implications for Wholesaler-Distributors

If commodity price growth returns to historic norms, then wholesaler-distributors are going to have to work harder for real growth. The revenue-enhancing benefit of product price inflation will dissipate as the growth in commodity prices eases. It will become harder for wholesaler-distributors to show top-line revenue growth, thus making volume growth more important as a source of revenue growth. Total gross margin dollars will shrink even if gross margin percent remains stable.

No wholesale distribution company has the power to influence overall commodity prices. Therefore, the best approach to this emerging trend is through the following careful monitoring of external trends and strategic preparation:

- **Analyze recent growth.** An over-reliance on inflation-boosted growth indicates that a revenue slowdown is coming to your company. Wholesale distribution executives should analyze the relative contributions of volume versus price growth to their companies' recent top-line revenue growth. How much would your top-line revenue growth slow down if product prices remain flat over the next 24 months?

- **Tighten inventory control.** Wholesaler-distributors can benefit from overall increases in prices by placing larger orders in advance of price increases. However, flat or declining prices create opposing dynamics in favor of leaner inventories. The demand-driven channel models described in Chapter Two will become much more important as commodity price growth slows.

- **Evaluate new profit sources.** Deflation wreaks havoc with the income statement of wholesaler-distributors that are *paid* for providing services to customers and suppliers in the supply chain in the form of gross margin. Product price deflation translates into fewer gross margin dollars to pay for the value that these services actually provide. Wholesale distribution executives should accelerate the development of fee-based services to avoid a profit squeeze caused by external pricing dynamics. (See Chapter Three.)

This concludes the major and emerging trends discussed in Part One. Part Two analyzes the results for three major markets in which wholesaler-distributors operate:

- Construction Markets
- Industrial and Commercial Markets
- Retail Consumer Markets.

Part Two
Detailed Results by Major Markets

Chapters Six through Eight present detailed results related to the major markets served by wholesaler-distributors:

Six Construction Markets
- Building Materials
- Contractor Supplies

Seven Industrial and Commercial Markets
- MRO Supplies (Industrial and Commercial)
- OEM and Production Materials

Eight Retail Consumer Markets
- Retail Stores and Dealers

Each chapter in Part Two contains the following sections:
- **Summary** highlighting the most important conclusions
- **Market Overview** presenting an industry overview and basic economic facts about each market
- **The Role of Wholesale Distribution** for each market
- **Analysis of the Major Trends** showing detailed results from the four trends in Part One.

Appendix C presents supplemental data about wholesaler-distributors of machinery and equipment products. Since wholesaler-distributors of these products operate across the three major markets, it is not meaningful to provide a separate market analysis.

CHAPTER SIX

Construction Markets

SUMMARY

Wholesaler-distributors of building materials and contractor supplies have shown consistent growth during the past 5 years due to strong residential construction activity, the rebound in commercial construction, and the growth of remodeling and repair work. The combination of many small customers and multiple specialties supports a diverse set of wholesale distribution lines of trade that are typically organized around product type.

The private label products trend will affect wholesaler-distributors of building materials much more than contractor supplies wholesaler-distributors. In contrast, the demand-driven channels trend will have a smaller impact on building materials markets than on any other market covered in this report. The impact on contractor supplies markets will be greater due in part to the connection to MRO markets. The consolidation of builders is changing wholesaler-distributors' profit sources and this creates new opportunities for both fee-based services to customers and fee-for-service logistics to suppliers. The fragmented nature of contractor markets suggests relatively fast penetration for the connected customers trend.

MARKET OVERVIEW

This section provides a brief overview of the construction industry and the major customer groups in this market—residential, nonresidential, and public construction, which are served by wholesaler-distributors.

Building Construction

Wholesaler-distributors sell to customers operating in all three major segments of the construction industry—residential, industrial/commercial (nonresidential), and public construction. Since these segments are somewhat counter cyclical to each other, they are rarely declining at the same time.

The residential home building industry has experienced a remarkable period of growth during the past 10 years. Single-family home starts exceeded 1.7 million new units in 2005, which is a 60% increase over the past decade. The residential housing boom has pushed the national home ownership rate to an historic high of 70%, with the largest percentage point gains coming from younger and minority households.

The home building industry became increasingly concentrated during the recent upturn. The market share of the top 10 builders doubled to 21% of closings in the past decade, with a few builders having even greater share in regional markets. This consolidation is expected to continue, especially as residential home building slows down. Nevertheless, small- and medium-volume builders continue to dominate smaller metro and rural areas.

Home builders are experiencing historically high profitability. The National Association of Home Builders estimates that 2006 operating profits of home builders will be 16%, compared to a range of 6%-8% throughout the 1990s.

Favorable demographic trends during the next 10 years will grow demand for housing across all age groups and sustain healthy spending on home improvements, according to forecasts by the Joint Center for Housing Studies of Harvard University.[29] The Center projects net household formations at 14.6 million during the next 10 years, which represents a 16% jump from the 12.6 million households added from 1995 to 2005.

Nonresidential construction, which contracted sharply in 2002, is growing at double-digit rates and will grow much faster than residential construction during the next few years. A major factor in this growth will be the construction of nursing homes and other residential homes for the growing elderly population, as well as health care facilities. Construction of schools will also grow, especially in the South and West where the population is growing the fastest.

Contractors

Specialty trade contractors account for 40% of the nearly $900 billion in total U.S. construction industry revenues and they represent about two out of three wage and salary jobs in the construction industry. The two largest specialized contractors account for 40% of all contractor locations—plumbing and HVAC contractors and electrical contractors.

In contrast to the home building segment, the contractor industry remains highly fragmented across many specialties and is dominated by small businesses. Despite attempts at consolidation within some specialties, more than 85% of contractors work in small businesses with fewer than 10 employees.

More than one-quarter of all construction workers are self-employed and perform work directly for property owners or act as contractors on small jobs. The highest rates of self-employment in construction are among painters and paperhangers (46%); carpet, floor, and tile installers and finishers (42%); and carpenters (33%).

The U.S. Bureau of Labor Statistics forecasts that total employment in many contractor occupations will grow faster in the next decade than the overall U.S. employment growth of 13% over the same period. (See Exhibit 6-1.) Other trends for contractors identified by the Bureau include the following:

- New job opportunities will be very good. Many contractors will be retiring, while fewer people with the right education or experience will be entering the skilled trades.

- Home improvement and repair construction will continue to grow faster than new home construction. Contractor employment will also grow faster in nonresidential construction over the coming decade.

- Remodeling should be the fastest growing sector of housing construction because of a growing stock of old residential and nonresidential buildings. Remodeling tends to be more labor-intensive than new construction.

- The construction industry will increasingly hire out the services of specialty trade workers instead of keeping these workers on their own payrolls.

Exhibit 6-1. Projected employment growth in contractor occupations, 2004 to 2014.

Occupation	Total U.S. Employment (000s), 2004	Percent Employed in Construction, 2004	Projected Growth, 2004 to 2014
Carpenters	1,349.0	55%	14%
Electricians	656.2	65%	12%
Pipelayers, Plumbers, Pipefitters, and Steamfitters	561.0	68%	15%
Painters and Paperhangers	485.6	41%	12%
Heating, Air Conditioning, and Refrigeration Mechanics and Installers	269.7	53%	19%
Cement Masons, Concrete Finishers, and Terrazzo Workers	207.9	89%	16%
Sheet Metal Workers	198.1	64%	12%
Drywall Installers, Ceiling Tile Installers, and Tapers	195.8	76%	8%
Carpet, Floor, and Tile Installers and Finishers	184.0	44%	13%
Brick Masons, Block Masons, and Stone Masons	176.8	65%	12%
Roofers	161.6	71%	17%

Source: U.S. Bureau of Labor Statistics, Occupational Employment Projections Program

THE ROLE OF WHOLESALE DISTRIBUTION

The combination of many small customers and multiple specialties supports a diverse set of wholesale distribution lines of trade that are typically organized around product type. Exhibit 6-2 highlights total distribution revenues in selected lines of trade serving this market.

This market includes two primary types of wholesaler-distributors. One-step distributors, often called *pro dealers*, sell primarily to builder and contractor end users. Two-step distributors sell primarily to retail outlets, such as building materials dealers, hardware stores, or lumberyards. Two-step distributors also include member-owned wholesaler co-ops.

Exhibit 6-2 shows substantial revenue to both contractors and retail stores for many subsectors of the market. Wholesaler-distributors sell certain products, such as roofing or plumbing products, primarily to contractors or builders. (See Exhibit 6-2, column 3.) Other products, such as lumber or hand tools, are also sold through two-step distribution by a wholesaler to a dealer or retailer. (See Exhibit 6-2, column 6.) Note that some of the wholesaler-distributor subsectors in Exhibit 6-2 also sell to MRO or OEM markets.

Wholesaler-distributors of building materials and contractor supplies have shown consistent growth during the past 5 years due to strong residential construction activity, the rebound in commercial construction, and the growth of remodeling and repair work. (See Exhibit 6-3.) Note that revenues of building materials distributors have benefited from product price inflation. For example, prices for building materials such as lumber products spiked in 2004 and remain above historic levels. In addition, the 22% revenue growth for building materials distributors translates to a lower, but still healthy, 11% after adjusting for inflation.

Looking forward, wholesaler-distributors in this market expect to see contractors and builders increasingly purchasing from manufacturers at the expense of the wholesale distribution channel. (See Exhibit 6-4). The pace of change is consistent with the forecasts presented in our 2004 report.

Purchases from retail home centers are an important factor in these markets, representing 15% and 10% of channel sales in 2006 for building materials and contractor supplies, respectively. These figures are forecasted to remain roughly stable over the next 5 years. Retail home centers have had difficulty growing their share of the professional contractor market, which is one important reason why The Home Depot has been aggressively acquiring wholesaler-distributors. (See Chapter Five for additional details.)

Exhibit 6-2. Total wholesaler-distributor revenues in selected lines of trade.

Line of Trade (defined by primary products)	Total Wholesaler-Distributor Revenues* (billions)	Share of Revenue by Market					
		Building Materials and Contractor Supplies	MRO Supplies (Industrial and Commercial)	OEM and Production Materials	Retail Stores and Dealers	Export Sales
BUILDING MATERIALS						
Plywood and Millwork	$49.1	45%	3%	9%	41%	1%
Lumber (without a Yard)	$25.1	29%	2%	11%	53%	5%
Roofing, Siding, and Insulation Materials	$20.3	79%	3%	1%	17%	1%
Lumber (with a Yard)	$19.2	17%	3%	11%	66%	3%
Floor Covering	$14.8	33%	9%	1%	57%	0%
Brick, Block, Tile, or Clay	$5.8	63%	3%	3%	30%	1%
Cement, Lime, and Related Products	$4.1	62%	5%	23%	9%	1%
Sand, Gravel, and Crushed Stone	$3.5	56%	7%	14%	23%	0%
Flat Glass and Other Construction Glass	$1.8	49%	9%	8%	30%	5%

Share of Revenue by Market

Line of Trade (defined by primary products)	Total Wholesaler-Distributor Revenues* (billions)	Building Materials and Contractor Supplies	MRO Supplies (Industrial and Commercial)	OEM and Production Materials	Retail Stores and Dealers	Export Sales
CONTRACTOR SUPPLIES						
Electrical Apparatus, Equipment, and Supplies	$70.9	39%	25%	23%	10%	3%
Forced Air Heating and Cooling Equipment and Supplies	$22.5	60%	10%	2%	26%	2%
Hand Tools, Hardware, and Fasteners	$33.8	15%	11%	19%	52%	3%
Plumbing and Hydronic Heating Equipment and Supplies	$27.2	56%	21%	6%	16%	1%
Refrigeration Equipment and Supplies	$5.8	34%	29%	11%	23%	4%

*July 2005 through June 2006
Figures do not add to 100% due to rounding.
Source: 2006 Wholesale Distribution Economic Reports. Latest data are available in 2007 Wholesale Distribution Economic Reports at www.nawpubs.org.

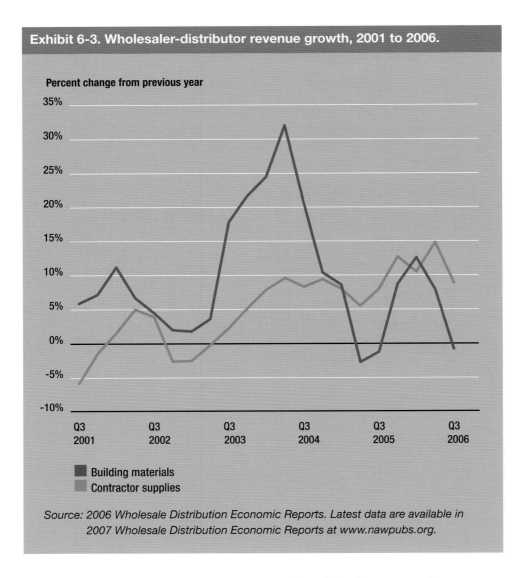

Exhibit 6-3. Wholesaler-distributor revenue growth, 2001 to 2006.

Percent change from previous year

Building materials
Contractor supplies

Source: 2006 Wholesale Distribution Economic Reports. Latest data are available in 2007 Wholesale Distribution Economic Reports at www.nawpubs.org.

A related challenge for two-step wholesaler sales will be the ongoing disappearance of smaller dealers and retailers, many of whom are unable to compete with home centers for the retail consumer or residential contractor. For example, the number of building materials dealer locations dropped by 5,600 (minus 13%) from 1998 to 2004. (See Exhibit 8-2.) Other specialty stores also have seen declines, such as hardware stores (down 7%), floor covering stores (down 6%), and paint stores (down 8%).

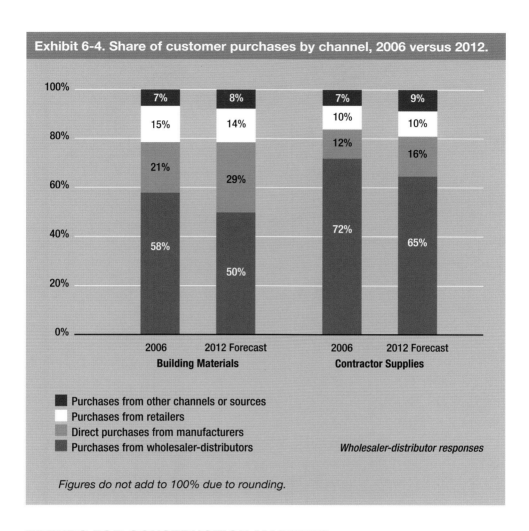

Exhibit 6-4. Share of customer purchases by channel, 2006 versus 2012.

Building Materials
- 2006: 7%, 15%, 21%, 58%
- 2012 Forecast: 8%, 14%, 29%, 50%

Contractor Supplies
- 2006: 7%, 10%, 12%, 72%
- 2012 Forecast: 9%, 10%, 16%, 65%

Legend:
- ■ Purchases from other channels or sources
- □ Purchases from retailers
- ▨ Direct purchases from manufacturers
- ▨ Purchases from wholesaler-distributors

Wholesaler-distributor responses

Figures do not add to 100% due to rounding.

TRENDS FOR CONSTRUCTION MARKETS

Trend 1: Private Label Products

The private label products trend will affect wholesaler-distributors of building materials very differently than contractor supplies. (See Exhibits 6-5 and 6-6.) Almost one-half of building materials wholesaler-distributors currently offer private label products, compared to only 23% of contractor supplies wholesaler-distributors. This gap will persist in the future.

These results reflect the significant product differences within the broader construction industry. Some building materials such as certain lumber products are globally priced commodities, and this makes it difficult for customers to ensure

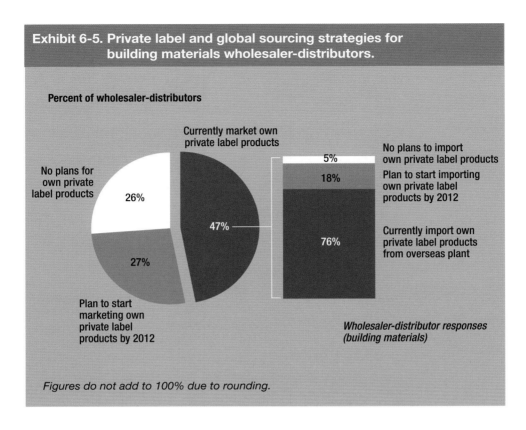

Exhibit 6-5. Private label and global sourcing strategies for building materials wholesaler-distributors.

Percent of wholesaler-distributors

Currently market own private label products

No plans for own private label products 26%

47%

27%

Plan to start marketing own private label products by 2012

No plans to import own private label products 5%

Plan to start importing own private label products by 2012 18%

Currently import own private label products from overseas plant 76%

Wholesaler-distributor responses (building materials)

Figures do not add to 100% due to rounding.

product quality. Wholesaler-distributors with strong corporate reputations and source loyalty can build their private label products.

For example, **Reid and Wright, Inc.** (www.reidwright.com), a distributor of redwood, cedar, and specialty building products, launched its own line of interior and exterior wood paneling and sidings in the mid 1990s. By creating its own "Signature Series" product, the company was able to provide customers with the right quality characteristics under one identifiable label, even though the actual products may come from different manufacturers. The product line allows the company to differentiate itself from large national lumber wholesalers. The ability to source from multiple manufacturers allows Reid and Wright to have higher availability than any single supplier because input products can be sourced from multiple sawmills.

In contrast, brand is a much more important factor for contractor supplies than for any other market. Some contractors use premium brands to communicate quality and reliability of their services to their customers, thereby increasing the importance of carrying high-quality brands.

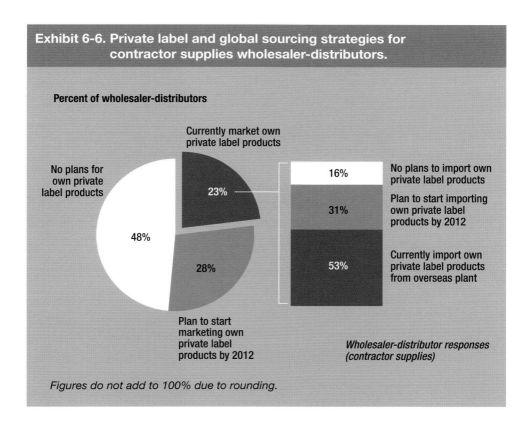

Exhibit 6-6. Private label and global sourcing strategies for contractor supplies wholesaler-distributors.

Percent of wholesaler-distributors

Currently market own private label products

No plans for own private label products

23%

48%

28%

Plan to start marketing own private label products by 2012

16% — No plans to import own private label products

31% — Plan to start importing own private label products by 2012

53% — Currently import own private label products from overseas plant

Wholesaler-distributor responses (contractor supplies)

Figures do not add to 100% due to rounding.

Contractor brand loyalty is derived from customer expectations. If a customer requests or specifies a brand, contractors are often obliged to provide that brand. The most important factors that drive customers to request specific brands include:

- Attempts to standardize purchases and rationalize vendors
- Product performance differences
- Situations where design, configuration, and performance measurement cause customers to invest more time to analyze product attributes
- Convenience (sometimes it is just easier to buy what has always been bought)
- Successful manufacturer marketing and promotional efforts aimed at building brand awareness or strength.

Product liability issues also limit the willingness of a distributor to enter certain categories. For example, power tools are less likely to have private brands, whereas plumbing fixtures and faucets have many private label product offerings.

Trend 2: Demand-Driven Channels

The demand-driven channels trend will have a smaller impact on building materials markets than on any other market covered in this report. The impact on contractor supplies markets will be greater, due in part to the connection to MRO markets, which are discussed in Chapter Seven.

Wholesaler-distributors of building materials are least likely to share data with their suppliers. (See Exhibit 6-7.) About 46% of wholesaler-distributors don't share point-of-sale data with suppliers, while another 41% only share data with a few key suppliers. More than one-third of these wholesaler-distributors also do not anticipate sharing any data by 2012. In contrast, wholesaler-distributors of contractor supplies are much more likely to share data in 2006 and in the future. (See Exhibit 6-8.)

The use of automatic product identification technologies is much lower in building materials versus contractor supplies. In 2006, only 32% of building materials wholesaler-distributors used bar codes, compared to 47% of contractor supplies wholesaler-distributors.

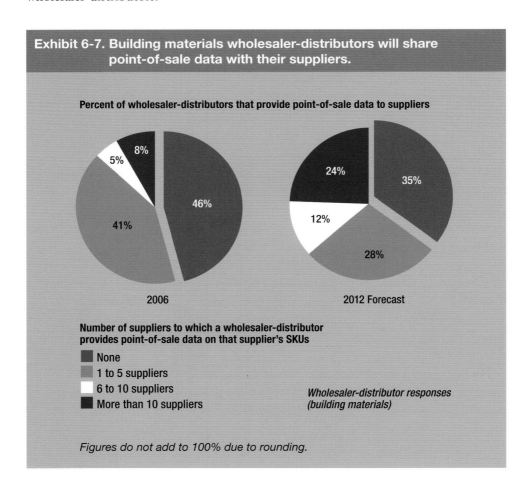

Exhibit 6-7. Building materials wholesaler-distributors will share point-of-sale data with their suppliers.

Percent of wholesaler-distributors that provide point-of-sale data to suppliers

2006

2012 Forecast

Number of suppliers to which a wholesaler-distributor provides point-of-sale data on that supplier's SKUs
- None
- 1 to 5 suppliers
- 6 to 10 suppliers
- More than 10 suppliers

Wholesaler-distributor responses (building materials)

Figures do not add to 100% due to rounding.

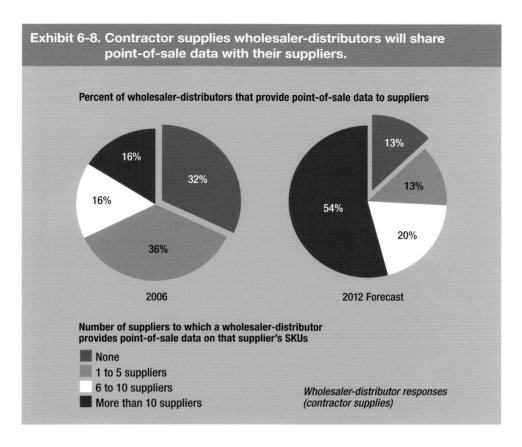

Exhibit 6-8. Contractor supplies wholesaler-distributors will share point-of-sale data with their suppliers.

Percent of wholesaler-distributors that provide point-of-sale data to suppliers

2006

2012 Forecast

Number of suppliers to which a wholesaler-distributor provides point-of-sale data on that supplier's SKUs

■ None
■ 1 to 5 suppliers
□ 6 to 10 suppliers
■ More than 10 suppliers

Wholesaler-distributor responses (contractor supplies)

The traditionally fragmented nature of customers in the construction markets, combined with the commodity nature of building materials products such as lumber and stone, make it difficult to bring demand-driven concepts to these markets. Small contractors purchase from a local distribution branch, a home center, or a local building materials dealer. Even when functioning as subcontractors to a builder or large customer, contractors have been the primary purchasers of materials for the job site.

Bid buying and the influence of other decision makers also limit the application of many traditional supply chain management techniques. The prevalence of bid buying by contractors generally limits opportunities for long-term collaboration and partnering. Contractors are hesitant to surrender negotiating leverage gained through quotations and they resist moving to a preferred supplier strategy.

However, manufacturer-suppliers in this market would benefit from better visibility to downstream demand, especially in the face of a residential construction slowdown. There has also been a proliferation of new products into the building materials industry during the recent construction boom, making sales forecasting harder and creating an even greater need for more accurate demand information. The bullwhip effect described in Chapter Two will lead to excess inventory at all stages of the building materials supply chain.

Thus, wholesaler-distributors that can apply demand-driven channel concepts to these markets will provide a new source of value for their suppliers, and perhaps will discover a new source of revenue. Right now, the potential for demand-driven channels in contractor supplies appears to be greater. The standards-setting initiative in the electrical industry represents a forward-thinking attempt to capture this opportunity. Plumbing wholesaler Barnett, discussed in the Action Ideas section of Chapter Two, provides another example of a wholesaler-distributor that has changed the game through innovation.

Trend 3: New Profit Models

Building materials wholesaler-distributors see less change to their current sources of gross margin than contractor supplies wholesaler-distributors. (See Exhibit 6-9.)

The role of fee-for-service payments represents one intriguing difference between the forecasts for building materials and contractor supplies. More than one-half (53%) of contractor supplies distributors expect fee-for-service payments from customers to be more important to gross margin. The consolidation of builders creates more service opportunities for these distributors because contractors are usually local providers unable to serve larger geographic areas.

New opportunities are emerging from selling installation services to builders, thereby reducing builders' construction labor needs and shifting accountability for any problems to distributors. **Eastway Supplies, Inc.** (www.EastwaySupplies.com), a PHCP (plumbing, heating, cooling, and piping) products distributor listed in Exhibit 3-7, installs shower doors and mirrors on a fee-based or contract basis. This service allows this company to derive a new profit stream from a builder beyond its typical wholesale business.

As large builders begin to transition from local sourcing to national purchasing contracts for building products, this creates opportunities for new relationships with the wholesale distribution channel. This trend will benefit larger wholesaler-distributors that can develop direct relationships with builders, supply products to local trade contractors in multiple regions, and help manage purchasing compliance.

For example, **Building Materials Holding Corporation** (www.bmhc.com) has added a range of construction services to its core business of lumber and building materials distribution. The company's SelectBuild division offers services targeted to high-volume production home builders, including project estimating, turnkey construction, millwork installation, rough framing assembly, and structural engineering.

Building materials distributors can credibly offer construction-related services because items such as framing lumber and cabinets equal 28% of the product costs

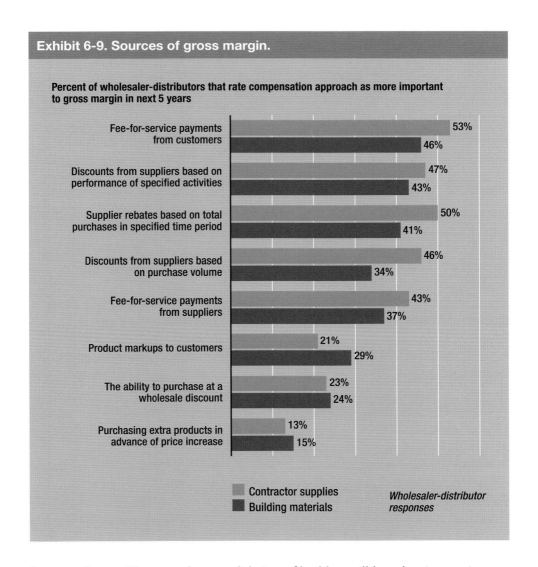

Exhibit 6-9. Sources of gross margin.

Percent of wholesaler-distributors that rate compensation approach as more important to gross margin in next 5 years

	Contractor supplies	Building materials
Fee-for-service payments from customers	53%	46%
Discounts from suppliers based on performance of specified activities	47%	43%
Supplier rebates based on total purchases in specified time period	50%	41%
Discounts from suppliers based on purchase volume	46%	34%
Fee-for-service payments from suppliers	43%	37%
Product markups to customers	21%	29%
The ability to purchase at a wholesale discount	23%	24%
Purchasing extra products in advance of price increase	13%	15%

■ Contractor supplies
■ Building materials

Wholesaler-distributor responses

for a new home. However, the consolidation of builders will have less intense impact on wholesaler-distributors of contractor supplies because these types of products are a small portion of residential construction. For example, the combination of electrical and HVAC products represent less than 7% of product costs for a new home. Therefore, contractors still have the ability to choose a product supplier for plumbing or electrical jobs; however, house frames are often preassembled by the lumber distributor and delivered to the job site ready for installation.

Fee-for-service logistics will also become more relevant in building materials and contractor supplies markets. Newly empowered large construction customers are shifting bids to a national level and away from geographically separate, regional markets. In some cases, they are dealing directly with manufacturers, which in turn are targeting large builders for national accounts. As we note in Chapter Three, wholesaler-distributors will evolve into logistics specialists for relationships when manufacturers handle national account management. The expected growth in fee-for-service payments from suppliers supports this evolution. (See Exhibit 6-9.)

Trend 4: Connected Customers

Although the construction industry tends to adopt technology more slowly than other industries, the fragmented nature of contractor markets suggests relatively fast penetration for technology connecting customers to each other.

Many small contractors are self-employed owner-operators who manage their businesses at night and on weekends, where they increasingly are likely to have high-speed Internet access. The coming generational transition highlighted by the U.S. Bureau of Labor Statistics, combined with the Internet's growing use as an information and communications tool, will accelerate the connected customers trend.

Many of the online forums shown in Exhibit 4-6 are very active, with participation from literally thousands of trade contractors who are looking for advice from their peers around the country. Consider **LawnSite.com**™ (www.lawnsite.com), an online forum for the lawn care and landscaping business. Many of the discussions are highly technical, such as the design of irrigation zones, comparisons of specific products for different landscape applications, and complex installation questions. Since so many companies in this industry are small or self-employed, they lack an internal network of peers. The Internet now allows these many small companies to combine their professional expertise and knowledge in a manner that was literally impossible 10 years ago.

A related trend is the growth of online rating services or forums written by the customers of wholesaler-distributors' customers. For example, wholesaler-distributors in the retail market should examine sites such as **Angie's List** (www.angieslist.com), which provides a way for consumers to rate the performance of local service providers in 70 cities around the United States. The company claims to receive 5,000 reports per month describing the service providers' time, prices, and quality of work. Participating as a *consumer* will allow a wholesale distribution executive to understand the real-world challenges facing customers and develop new services that help his/her customers to succeed.

As we found in the 2004 report, customers in construction markets are slowly adopting online ordering. Distributors selling to contractors expect to receive about 30% of their sales revenues electronically by 2012. (See Exhibit 6-10.) The fastest growth will occur in orders placed directly on a wholesaler-distributor's Web site. Orders received by mail, phone, or fax will drop by about 13% for both building materials and contractor supplies.

Exhibit 6-10. A wholesaler-distributor's sales revenue by customer ordering method, 2006 versus 2012.

	Percent of a Wholesaler-Distributor's Sales Revenue	
Building Materials	**2006**	**2012**
TRADITIONAL ORDERING METHODS		
Mail, telephone, or fax	61%	48%
Walk-in and counter sales	8%	7%
Face-to-face with sales representative	20%	15%
Subtotal	*89%*	*70%*
ONLINE ORDERING METHODS		
E-mail sent to your company	4%	9%
Online via wholesaler-distributor's Web site	2%	11%
Online via third-party Web site	1%	2%
Via Electronic Data Interchange (EDI)	4%	9%
Subtotal	*11%*	*31%*
Total	**100%**	**100%**

	Percent of a Wholesaler-Distributor's Sales Revenue	
Contractor Supplies	**2006**	**2012**
TRADITIONAL ORDERING METHODS		
Mail, telephone, or fax	52%	38%
Walk-in and counter sales	22%	20%
Face-to-face with sales representative	15%	12%
Subtotal	*89%*	*70%*
ONLINE ORDERING METHODS		
E-mail sent to your company	4%	11%
Online via wholesaler-distributor's Web site	2%	12%
Online via third-party Web site	0%	1%
Via Electronic Data Interchange (EDI)	4%	7%
Subtotal	*10%*	*31%*
Total	**100%**	**100%**

Wholesaler-distributor responses

Figures do not add to 100% due to rounding.

There are some interesting differences between wholesaler-distributors focusing on contractor supplies versus building materials:

- Orders by e-mail will increase by 7% for contractor supplies wholesaler-distributors versus a 5% increase for building materials wholesaler-distributors. This difference highlights the importance of *always on access* for distributors that sell to smaller, more fragmented customers.

- About 58% of building materials wholesaler-distributors expect most customers to ask them to match prices found on the Internet, compared to 74% of contractor supplies wholesaler-distributors. Contractor supplies products are easier to compare online and can be shipped by common carrier. (See the Bosch Power Tools example in Chapter Four.)

- These customers are also among the most likely to use online forums to gather information and compare notes with other contractors. The small size of contractor companies and the large number of self-employed contractors drive this desire for connection. Some of the most active online forums shown in Exhibit 4-6 cater to trade contractors.

Product characteristics and applications also highlight an important difference between future sales methods for building materials versus contractor supplies. Walk-in and counter sales will remain about 20% of contractor supplies purchases and about 8% of building materials purchases. Contractors purchasing products for repair need materials right away for pickup or same-day delivery, whereas often heavier building materials are ordered in advance and delivered to a job site.

CHAPTER SEVEN

Industrial and Commercial Markets

SUMMARY

Domestic manufacturing continues to undergo a dramatic transformation, which challenges industrial MRO and OEM wholesaler-distributors. Manufacturing employment has not rebounded following the unprecedented decline that began in 2000. In contrast, the commercial MRO business is much less cyclical than the industrial business because it is tied to many diverse segments of the U.S. economy.

The private label products trend is well established in both MRO and OEM markets. Almost one-half of MRO supplies distributors and nearly two-thirds of OEM and production materials distributors currently offer private label products. Demand-driven channels are coming to industrial and commercial wholesale distribution markets. By 2012, many MRO supplies distributors and OEM and production materials distributors expect to share point-of-sale data with suppliers.

Distribution executives in industrial and commercial markets expect important shifts in the composition of their gross margin. The shift to manufacturer-led compensation is most pronounced in OEM and production materials markets, whereas MRO supplies distributors are benefiting from fee-for-service offerings to customers. The Internet will grow to be a crucial sourcing tool in these markets, although the growth rates in Web site ordering have slowed in the past few years.

MARKET OVERVIEW

This section provides a brief overview of industrial manufacturing and commercial facilities markets, which contain the major customers for MRO and OEM products sold by wholesaler-distributors.

Industrial Manufacturing

The fortunes of wholesaler-distributors of MRO and OEM products to industrial plants are more closely tied to the industrial manufacturing economy than to any other wholesale distribution sector. These two sets of products are often complementary in usage inside manufacturing facilities. OEM products are machinery, supplies, and components that are used to produce the end product. MRO products are those that are needed to keep the organization and machinery functional and productive.

Manufacturing capacity utilization is now running above 80%, and this is up substantially from the 20-year low of 72% reached in 2001. Net profits of manufacturers have been rising by nearly 9% a year since the last recession. Many economists expect capacity utilization to remain at this level through 2007, suggesting increased capital investment and continued growth for industrial distributors. Production is growing fastest for manufacturers of business equipment, such as computers, electrical, and defense equipment.

Despite this recent turnaround, domestic manufacturing continues to undergo a dramatic transformation. Manufacturing employment has not rebounded following the unprecedented decline that began in 2000. The period from 1998 to 2004 saw a net loss of 27,000 manufacturing plants (7% of the 1998 total) and more than 3 million domestic manufacturing jobs (18% of the 1998 total). (See Exhibit 7-1.) Some sectors were hit particularly hard. Fabricated metal products, which represents one out of six (17%) U.S. plants, lost 4,000 plants and 250,000 workers.

The long-term loss of a domestic manufacturing base has hit industrial distribution hard. *Industrial Distribution's The 60th Annual Survey of Distributor Operations*[30] found that 4 out of 10 industrial distributors report having customer operations moved to China within the past 2 years. The average industrial distributor lost 9.2% of sales from no longer being able to sell to those customers. Smaller distributors have been hit hardest, losing an average of 12.5% of sales. Two-thirds of industrial distributors expect that even more of their customers' operations will move to China within the next 3 years.

Surviving manufacturers are using a variety of strategies to remain viable, such as flexible manufacturing systems, shorter productions runs, complex value-added assembly, and more intensive use of information technology. Forecasts by the U.S.

Bureau of Labor Statistics suggest a much slower rate of job losses in the future, with the exception of textile and apparel sectors. (See Exhibit 7-1, column 6.) Total job losses through 2012 are forecasted to be only 624,000 or 4% compared to the baseline year of 2004. Job losses, excluding apparel and textiles, are forecasted to be only 390,000. Unfortunately, equivalent forecasts for the number of manufacturing plants are not available.

The competitive pressures on manufacturing are also leading to a major surge in productivity. Output per hour among employees in durable goods manufacturing has more than doubled in the past 14 years. Output per hour among employees in nondurable goods manufacturing has increased half as fast, a still impressive 49%. (See Exhibit 7-2.) Output per hour, the most commonly cited labor productivity statistic, captures the combined effect of changes in technology, capital per worker, level of output, capacity utilization, managerial skill, and many other factors.

As manufacturing gets more complex and companies look for further productivity gains, manufacturers report moderate to severe shortages of qualified, skilled production employees. Research by the National Association of Manufacturers[31] found that:

- About 90% of manufacturing executives indicate a moderate to severe shortage of qualified, skilled production employees. This result does not vary significantly when controlling for size, industry segment, or region.

- Approximately 65% of all respondents and 74% of respondents with more than 500 employees reported a moderate to severe shortage of scientists and engineers. This shortage is even more acute for certain industry segments such as aerospace and defense, with 80% of respondents indicating a moderate to severe shortage.

- What is more, 39% of respondents also indicated a moderate to severe shortage of qualified, unskilled production employees.

Most significantly, more than one-half of all manufacturing executives indicated that the shortage of available skills has had a negative impact on their ability to serve customers. While troubling for the manufacturing sector, these pressures provide opportunities for wholesaler-distributors to offer services that improve the productivity of manufacturing employees.

Exhibit 7-1. U.S. manufacturing plants and employment.

| Product | Number of Plants | | Employment | | |
	Number of Plants, 2004	Actual Percent Change, 1998 to 2004	Number of Workers (000s), 2004	Actual Percent Change, 1998 to 2004	Projected Percent Change, 2004 to 2012
Printing and Related Support Activities	35,320	-16%	662.6	-20%	-8%
Apparel	12,310	-29%	285.5	-55%	-52%
Fabricated Metal Products	59,370	-6%	1,497.1	-14%	-1%
Machinery	27,040	-12%	1,143.0	-24%	-10%
Computer and Electronic Products	15,100	-14%	1,322.8	-28%	-6%
Plastics and Rubber Products	14,890	-11%	805.7	-15%	-7%
Textile Mills	3,640	-22%	236.9	-44%	-42%
Food	26,770	-4%	1,493.7	-4%	3%
Wood Products	16,780	-5%	549.6	-10%	6%
Electrical Equipment, Appliances and Components	6,290	-12%	445.1	-25%	-15%
Paper	5,420	-9%	495.5	-21%	-2%
Transportation Equipment	12,710	-4%	1,765.7	-15%	4%
Leather and Allied Products	1,480	-18%	41.8	-50%	-19%
Chemicals	13,360	-2%	887.0	-11%	-1%

	Number of Plants		Employment		
Product	Number of Plants, 2004	Actual Percent Change, 1998 to 2004	Number of Workers (000s), 2004	Actual Percent Change, 1998 to 2004	Projected Percent Change, 2004 to 2012
Primary Metals	5,430	-1%	466.8	-27%	-15%
Textile Product Mills	7,120	0%	175.7	-19%	-15%
Miscellaneous	31,800	0%	655.5	-10%	-2%
Nonmetallic Mineral Products	16,710	1%	505.5	-6%	3%
Petroleum and Coal Products	2,460	11%	111.7	-17%	-11%
Beverage and Tobacco Products	3,360	23%	194.6	-7%	-5%
Furniture	21,740	5%	573.3	-11%	-1%
Total	**339,100**	**-7%**	**14,315.1**	**-18%**	**-4%**

Source: U.S. Bureau of Labor Statistics; U.S. Census Bureau

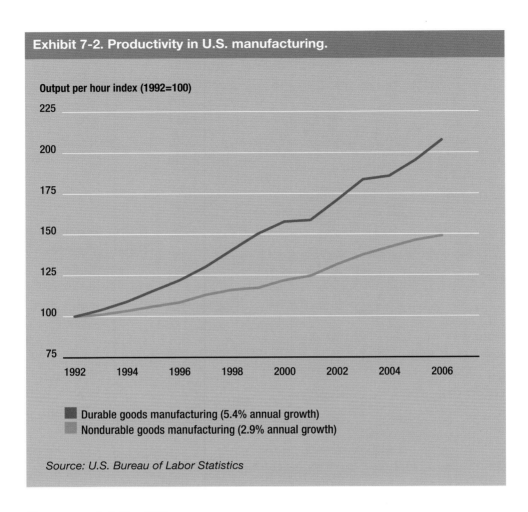

Exhibit 7-2. Productivity in U.S. manufacturing.

Output per hour index (1992=100)

■ Durable goods manufacturing (5.4% annual growth)
■ Nondurable goods manufacturing (2.9% annual growth)

Source: U.S. Bureau of Labor Statistics

Commercial Facilities

The wholesale distribution of MRO products outside of industrial customers encompasses a wide range of products used for the maintenance, repair, operations, and remodeling of many different types of facilities.

The commercial MRO business is much less cyclical than the industrial business because it is tied to many diverse segments of the U.S. economy. For example, commercial MRO customers purchase products for the maintenance, repair, operations, and remodeling of many different types of nonindustrial facilities, such as multiple-family housing, schools, hospitals, and hotels.

Nonindustrial facilities typically contain service-based businesses for which product purchases are a much smaller percent of sales dollars. For example, the CAPS Research (www.capsresearch.org) benchmarking program estimates that total purchasing spend as a percentage of sales dollars is 17% in financial services, which is one of the largest employers in commercial office buildings, versus 57% in industrial manufacturing.

The diversity of nonindustrial, commercial facilities precludes a more complete description of this diverse segment.

THE ROLE OF WHOLESALE DISTRIBUTION

Exhibit 7-3 summarizes total wholesale distribution revenues for diverse lines of trade serving the MRO market. Note that a few of the wholesale distribution subsectors shown in Exhibit 6-2, such as electrical or plumbing products, also have important sales in industrial and commercial MRO markets.

Purchases from wholesaler-distributors are expected to trend downward for both OEM and MRO customers. The trend is not a revolutionary shift, but rather a gradual shift of channel share over the next 5 years. For distributors selling OEM products, customers will increase direct purchases from manufacturers rather than seek alternative channels. (See Exhibit 7-4.) Domestic manufacturers purchasing OEM products face global competition built on low-cost production and supply chain economics. Visibility to long-term production runs and the use of collaborative forecasting and replenishment dampen the need for local on-hand safety stock.

MRO supplies are partially protected from this trend. The high proportion of nonstock (unplanned) MRO purchases and a large number of potential MRO suppliers prohibit customers from considering direct relationship options, thereby favoring a channel that can consolidate vendors.

Exhibit 7-3. Total wholesaler-distributor revenues in selected lines of trade.

Line of Trade (defined by primary products)	Total Wholesaler-Distributor Revenues* (billions)	Share of Revenue by Market				
		Building Materials and Contractor Supplies	MRO Supplies (Industrial and Commercial)	OEM and Production Materials	Retail Stores and Dealers	Export Sales
MRO EMPHASIS**						
Surgical, Medical, and Hospital Equipment and Supplies	$54.8	1%	85%	0%	11%	3%
Industrial and Personal Service Paper	$35.2	1%	23%	24%	46%	5%
Stationery and Office Supplies	$32.1	0%	59%	2%	39%	1%
Aircraft and Aeronautical Equipment and Supplies	$26.5	0%	62%	8%	4%	26%
Printing and Writing Paper	$26.3	2%	34%	30%	29%	6%
Paint and Paint Supplies	$6.7	9%	37%	16%	36%	2%
Dental Equipment and Supplies	$6.7	0%	90%	0%	7%	3%
OEM EMPHASIS						
Metal Service Centers	$130.4	17%	15%	59%	3%	5%
Agricultural Products Wholesaler-Distributors	$112.3	0%	3%	42%	3%	52%
Electronic Components and Parts	$89.0	1%	9%	65%	14%	11%

	Total Wholesaler-Distributor Revenues* (billions)	Share of Revenue by Market				
Line of Trade (defined by primary products)		Building Materials and Contractor Supplies	MRO Supplies (Industrial and Commercial)	OEM and Production Materials	Retail Stores and Dealers	Export Sales
Chemicals and Allied Products	$66.0	2%	17%	64%	5%	11%
Agricultural Chemicals and Fertilizers	$51.6	1%	3%	52%	31%	13%
Plastics Materials and Basic Shapes	$21.0	11%	10%	65%	5%	9%
General Line Industrial MRO Supplies	$15.0	7%	17%	68%	7%	2%
Mechanical Power Transmission (Bearings) Supplies	$8.3	5%	18%	66%	8%	3%
Nonlumber Forest Products	$8.1	1%	10%	47%	5%	38%
Industrial Valves and Fittings (except Fluid Power)	$7.9	25%	16%	50%	6%	3%
Industrial Containers and Supplies	$7.8	1%	9%	67%	20%	3%
Welding Supplies	$4.3	12%	16%	49%	21%	2%
Industrial Gases	$3.5	10%	33%	43%	13%	1%

* July 2005 through June 2006
** See Exhibit 6-2 for additional MRO subsectors.
Figures do not add to 100% due to rounding.
Source: 2006 Wholesale Distribution Economic Reports. Latest data are available in 2007 Wholesale Distribution Economic Reports
at www.nawpubs.org.

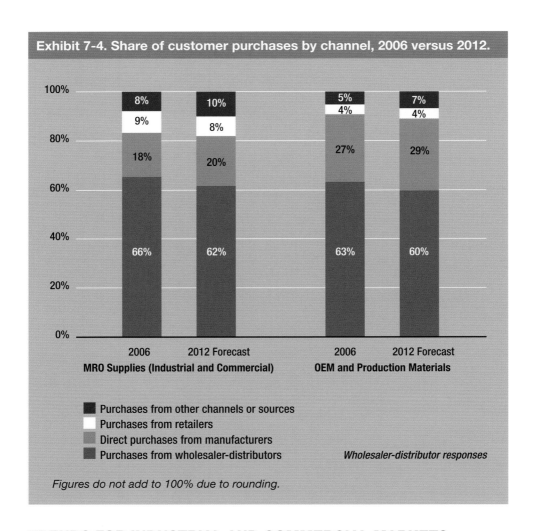

Exhibit 7-4. Share of customer purchases by channel, 2006 versus 2012.

MRO Supplies (Industrial and Commercial)
- 2006: 8%, 9%, 18%, 66%
- 2012 Forecast: 10%, 8%, 20%, 62%

OEM and Production Materials
- 2006: 5%, 4%, 27%, 63%
- 2012 Forecast: 7%, 4%, 29%, 60%

Legend:
- ■ Purchases from other channels or sources
- □ Purchases from retailers
- ▨ Direct purchases from manufacturers
- ▨ Purchases from wholesaler-distributors

Wholesaler-distributor responses

Figures do not add to 100% due to rounding.

TRENDS FOR INDUSTRIAL AND COMMERCIAL MARKETS

Trend 1: Private Label Products

The private label products trend is well established in both MRO and OEM markets (See Exhibits 7-5 and 7-6.) Almost one-half of MRO supplies distributors and nearly two-thirds of OEM and production materials distributors currently offer private label products. OEM and production materials distributors are also more likely to source products from overseas.

These results point to the new value proposition for intermediaries in these markets. As customers shop for the lowest price and highest value provider, products will become increasingly commoditized. Distributors have an opportunity to provide alternative products and help customers with sourcing, instead of only providing a sales channel for branded manufacturers.

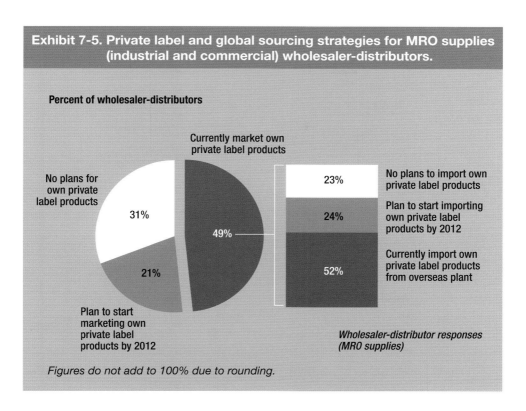

Exhibit 7-5. Private label and global sourcing strategies for MRO supplies (industrial and commercial) wholesaler-distributors.

Percent of wholesaler-distributors

Currently market own private label products

No plans for own private label products — 31%

49%

21%

Plan to start marketing own private label products by 2012

No plans to import own private label products — 23%

Plan to start importing own private label products by 2012 — 24%

Currently import own private label products from overseas plant — 52%

Wholesaler-distributor responses (MRO supplies)

Figures do not add to 100% due to rounding.

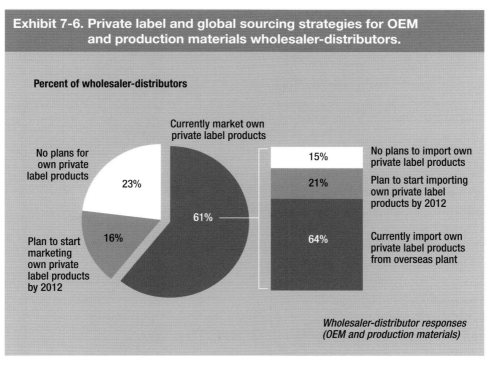

Exhibit 7-6. Private label and global sourcing strategies for OEM and production materials wholesaler-distributors.

Percent of wholesaler-distributors

Currently market own private label products

No plans for own private label products — 23%

61%

16%

Plan to start marketing own private label products by 2012

No plans to import own private label products — 15%

Plan to start importing own private label products by 2012 — 21%

Currently import own private label products from overseas plant — 64%

Wholesaler-distributor responses (OEM and production materials)

A wide variety of private label examples were mentioned during our research by executives at MRO and OEM wholesaler-distributors, including:

- Bright copy paper
- Carbide round tools
- Chemicals
- Electric terminals
- Floor care products
- Laundry dispensing products
- Mechanical wedge anchors
- Molded or extruded shapes
- Privately branded hose
- Spray foam insulation.

The potential for private label products is greater in MRO and OEM markets than in markets where brand plays a more important role, such as contractor supplies. Based on our interviews, some MRO supplies distributors focus private brands on commodity-type products, which provide a workable, competitive item for consumption. Others focus on developing a range of products, some of which may be premium brands. Arbill Safety Products, whose strategy is described in the Action Ideas section of Chapter One, is an example of the latter strategy.

Trend 2: Demand-Driven Channels

Demand-driven channels are coming to industrial and commercial wholesale distribution markets. By 2012, 36% of MRO supplies wholesaler-distributors and 44% of OEM and production materials wholesaler-distributors expect to be sharing point-of-sale data with more than 10 suppliers. (See Exhibits 7-7 and 7-8.)

The lower figure for MRO supplies reflects the challenges in building true downstream visibility in demand-driven channels for these products. Customers often have short purchasing horizons geared toward the current job and current day's work. They need materials right away for pickup or same-day delivery. An industrial facility that requires maintenance or repair needs immediate service so that it does not suffer lost production time. Customers tend to deal with only a few reliable suppliers that can be counted on to deliver a wide range of products with straightforward billing.

Nevertheless, demand-driven channels will expand, especially for wholesaler-distributors selling to industrial buyers. Centralized purchasing is already an established practice at many industrial companies, leading to fewer spot buys of MRO products. The strategic sourcing trend described in our 2004 report and summarized briefly in Chapter One in this report provides industrial purchasing managers with visibility to actual usage and consumption within their own organizations.

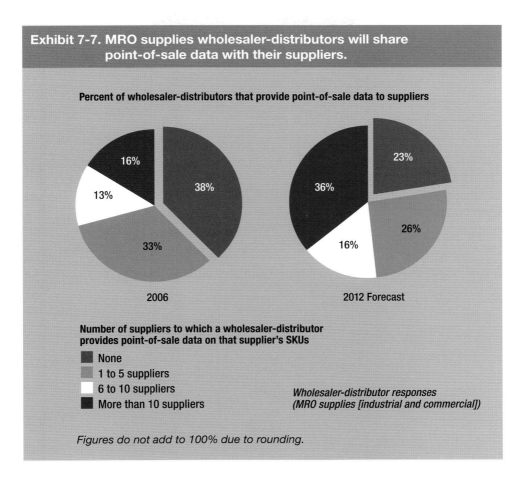

Exhibit 7-7. MRO supplies wholesaler-distributors will share point-of-sale data with their suppliers.

Percent of wholesaler-distributors that provide point-of-sale data to suppliers

16%
13%
38%
33%

23%
36%
26%
16%

2006

2012 Forecast

Number of suppliers to which a wholesaler-distributor provides point-of-sale data on that supplier's SKUs

■ None
■ 1 to 5 suppliers
□ 6 to 10 suppliers
■ More than 10 suppliers

*Wholesaler-distributor responses
(MRO supplies [industrial and commercial])*

Figures do not add to 100% due to rounding.

Other key enabling factors for demand-driven channels are present in these markets. Wholesaler-distributors in MRO and OEM markets have visibility into customer demand due to the prevalence of VMI arrangements. (See Exhibit 2-3.) Almost one-half of MRO supplies distributors use bar coding in their operations, which is the second highest adoption rate of any market studied in this report, except for retail channels.

The complexity of some OEM and production materials channels presents a barrier to adoption of demand-driven channels. A simple one-step system of manufacturer/distributor/customer is less common than in MRO channels. Although the OEM customer orders directly from the manufacturer for some products, many products are assembled and worked on by third-, second-, and first-tier suppliers. This means that information and coordination need to extend up through multiple layers of the customer's supply chain. Ironically, this multiple-level complexity also increases the potential for bullwhip effects.

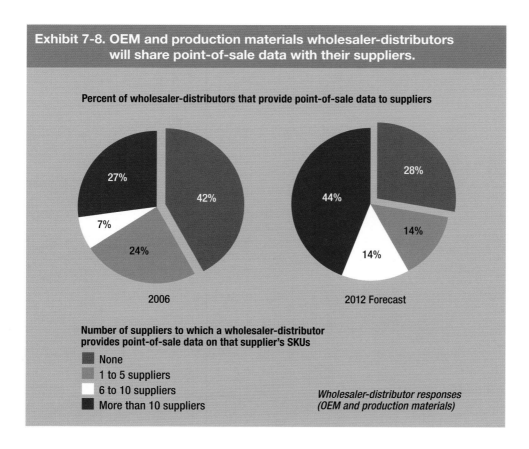

Exhibit 7-8. OEM and production materials wholesaler-distributors will share point-of-sale data with their suppliers.

Percent of wholesaler-distributors that provide point-of-sale data to suppliers

27% 42% 7% 24%

2006

28% 44% 14% 14%

2012 Forecast

Number of suppliers to which a wholesaler-distributor provides point-of-sale data on that supplier's SKUs

- None
- 1 to 5 suppliers
- 6 to 10 suppliers
- More than 10 suppliers

Wholesaler-distributor responses (OEM and production materials)

Trend 3: New Profit Models

Wholesale distribution executives in OEM and MRO markets expect their companies to see important shifts in the composition of their gross margin. (See Exhibit 7-9.)

The shift to manufacturer-led compensation is most pronounced in OEM and production materials markets. Fee-based services related to contract manufacturing on behalf of suppliers has emerged as an established practice for OEM industrial products, and this was a prediction made in the 2004 report.

It is surprising to see two particular channel compensation elements—supplier discounts based on purchase volume and forward buying in advance of a price increase—among wholesaler-distributors of OEM and production materials. Both factors contribute to bullwhip effects, as we discuss in the first section of Chapter Two. The growth of these two factors is especially noticeable given the tendency for more complex OEM channels to experience bullwhip effects in the supply chain.

The growth of fee-for-service offerings to customers is consistent with projections made in the 2004 report. Prominent services for MRO markets include tool crib management, storeroom management, and other related on-site inventory management services.

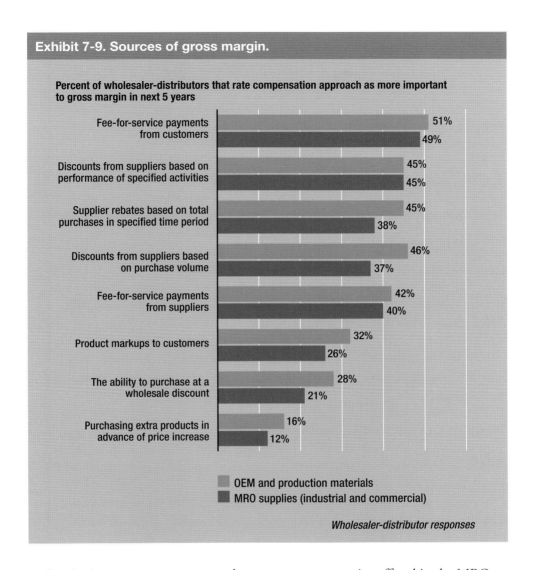

Exhibit 7-9. Sources of gross margin.

Percent of wholesaler-distributors that rate compensation approach as more important to gross margin in next 5 years

	OEM and production materials	MRO supplies (industrial and commercial)
Fee-for-service payments from customers	51%	49%
Discounts from suppliers based on performance of specified activities	45%	45%
Supplier rebates based on total purchases in specified time period	45%	38%
Discounts from suppliers based on purchase volume	46%	37%
Fee-for-service payments from suppliers	42%	40%
Product markups to customers	32%	26%
The ability to purchase at a wholesale discount	28%	21%
Purchasing extra products in advance of price increase	16%	12%

Wholesaler-distributor responses

On-site inventory management, the most common service offered in the MRO supplies market, provides an operational version of strategic sourcing aimed at the traditional plant-level buyer of industrial products. Distributors providing integrated supply act as the outsourced purchasing department for an individual location. The plant forfeits responsibility for indirect materials and can deal with one supplier for all its needs.

When the distributor runs the on-site stockrooms or tool crib, the plant manager sees business benefits, such as better purchasing power, increased stock fill rates, improved customer service, and reduced stockroom employee turnover. Once plant-level customers recognized the value of this offer, distributors earned respectable returns by emphasizing service-level agreements and fee-based compensation instead of simple product price reductions. Given these realities, distributors offering integrated supply should recognize their unique value in the strategic sourcing value chain; that is, they provide the *last mile* of fulfillment to the customer.

An executive at a distributor of industrial MRO supplies said: "I believe that in the next 5 years, there will be a continuation of vendor reduction by our customers. They will use integrated supply through major integrators and alliances to accomplish their goals. The ultimate goal in this strategy is to outsource the procurement, inventory, and order processing of all MRO products."

As highlighted in Chapter Three, a challenge to future success will be the mindset of wholesale distribution executives. Some distributors lack a culture of getting paid for advice instead of simply being paid with gross margin dollars from a product order. One distribution executive remarked: "We don't offer advice to customers unless it helps us make more money." This all-too-common view does not reflect a modern view of professional services, as discussed in the Action Ideas section of Chapter Three.

An executive at a fluid power and motion control distributor expressed a more forward-thinking viewpoint: "The next 5 years will be an excellent sales growth time for companies that adapt to the needs of customers: Vendor-managed inventory, vendor-managed maintenance, in-plant engineering, and technical support will all be areas of growth opportunities. It will be an exciting and challenging time. We plan to adapt product offerings with technical expertise to a decreasing manufacturing base."

Trend 4: Connected Customers

The use of technology for sourcing and purchasing will continue to grow in the OEM and MRO markets, although there are some important differences between these two groups.

In particular, industrial OEM buyers will adopt online tools for their interactions with distributors, driven by the need for efficiencies and growing sophistication. However, buyers of MRO supplies will adopt online ordering more slowly. These results reflect the fact that the MRO market has now broadened beyond industrial plants to include the less cyclical commercial MRO business.

Many industrial buyers use the Internet as their first step when sourcing products and services, as we note in Chapter Four. According to our survey, 45% of the customers of OEM and production materials wholesaler-distributors will go online to get product information by 2012, up from 21% of customers in 2006. The figures for customers of MRO supplies are slightly lower—13% in 2006, growing to 37% by 2012.

The prevalence of online reverse auctions, particularly in OEM and production materials markets, reflects the Internet's role as a sourcing tool. Reverse auctions are real-time price competitions between prequalified suppliers to win a customer's business. These auctions occur over the Internet using specialized software. Bidders, who could be either distributors or suppliers to distributors, submit progressively lower priced bids during the scheduled auction time. Unlike a traditional auction in which prices are bid higher, the winner of a reverse auction is the company that submits the lowest bid.

Only 3% of OEM and production materials wholesaler-distributors face reverse auctions from most customers in 2006 versus 6% of MRO supplies wholesaler-distributors. (See Exhibit 7-10.)

However, OEM and production materials wholesaler-distributors expect much faster growth over the next 5 years. This difference reflects the relative ease of conducting auctions when products or services can be translated into clearly defined attributes and unambiguous specifications for production materials.

The CAPS Research (www.capsresearch.org) benchmarking program estimates that 2% to 4% of purchasing occurred via online auctions in 2006. Industries with higher than average spend via online auction include electronics and food manufacturing.

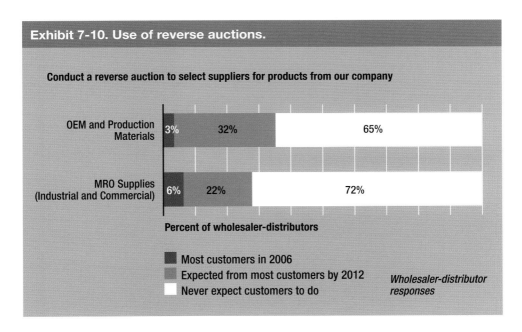

Exhibit 7-10. Use of reverse auctions.

Online ordering will continue to grow dramatically, especially for orders placed directly on a wholesaler-distributor's Web site instead of by phone or fax. (See Exhibit 7-11.) While traditional methods still account for more than 80% of all orders, wholesale distribution executives project dramatic growth in online orders via any method (Web, e-mail, EDI) to represent approximately 40% of orders.

Unlike the markets described in Chapters Six and Eight, the growth rates of Web site ordering have slowed since our last survey in the 2004 report. For example:

- In 2003, we found that Web orders to MRO distributors were estimated to represent only 2% of a wholesaler-distributor's sales revenue in 2003 and forecast to grow to 15% by 2008. However, Web orders were only 3% of revenue in 2006 and forecast to increase to only 13% by 2012.

- In 2003, we found that Web orders to OEM distributors were estimated to represent only 2% of a wholesaler-distributor's sales revenue in 2003 and forecast to grow to 13% by 2008. However, Web orders were only 5% of revenue in 2006 and forecast to increase to 18% by 2012.

Walk-in and counter sales will remain a small but crucial portion of MRO distributors' business for customers with urgent repair needs. In contrast, in-person orders placed through an outside sales rep will be somewhat higher for OEM products than for MRO products.

Exhibit 7-11. A wholesaler-distributor's sales revenue by customer ordering method, 2006 versus 2012.

	Percent of a Wholesaler-Distributor's Sales Revenue	
MRO Supplies (Industrial and Commercial)	2006	2012
TRADITIONAL ORDERING METHODS		
Mail, telephone, or fax	56%	40%
Walk-in and counter sales	6%	5%
Face-to-face with sales representative	21%	17%
Subtotal	*83%*	*62%*
ONLINE ORDERING METHODS		
E-mail sent to your company	6%	12%
Online via wholesaler-distributor's Web site	3%	13%
Online via third-party Web site	1%	2%
Via Electronic Data Interchange (EDI)	7%	11%
Subtotal	*17%*	*38%*
Total	**100%**	**100%**

	Percent of a Wholesaler-Distributor's Sales Revenue	
OEM and Production Materials	2006	2012
TRADITIONAL ORDERING METHODS		
Mail, telephone, or fax	67%	48%
Walk-in and counter sales	3%	2%
Face-to-face with sales representative	14%	9%
Subtotal	*84%*	*59%*
ONLINE ORDERING METHODS		
E-mail sent to your company	7%	14%
Online via wholesaler-distributor's Web site	5%	18%
Online via third-party Web site	0%	1%
Via Electronic Data Interchange (EDI)	3%	9%
Subtotal	*15%*	*42%*
Total	**100%**	**100%**

Wholesaler-distributor responses

Figures do not add to 100% due to rounding.

CHAPTER EIGHT

Retail Consumer Markets

SUMMARY

Retail sectors are becoming more concentrated and increasingly dominated by a handful of large, multiple-location chain stores, warehouse clubs, home centers, and supercenters. Wholesaler-distributors serving retail markets face a shrinking number of potential customers even though overall retail sales continue to expand. As a result, more than one-half of wholesaler-distributors in retail markets offer private label products, which often provide unique products to help their small retail customers compete against the retail giants.

Wholesaler-distributors in retail markets share data with more suppliers than in other markets, and this reflects the fact that the demand-driven concept originated in retail industries. Similar to other markets, wholesaler-distributors in retail markets expect that manufacturers will take on more responsibility for a wholesaler-distributor's profit margin from product distribution. However, fee-for-service payments from customers will be harder to get than in other markets. Online ordering will see substantial growth, while ordering methods that are still termed *traditional* in other customer segments will see a sustained decline.

MARKET OVERVIEW

This sector of the wholesale distribution industry includes primarily finished products that ultimately will be resold to household consumers. Wholesaler-distributor revenues in this sector are higher than in other parts of the distribution industry because the value of many inputs has been added throughout the supply chain, whereas the construction, MRO, and OEM markets represent the wholesale distribution of intermediate goods.

Finished Retail Goods

U.S. retail and foodservice sales were $4.1 trillion in 2005. (See Exhibit 8-1.) Total sales were $3.2 trillion, excluding automobiles, the single largest category. Since retail markets are consumer-oriented, the size of each subsegment is ultimately determined by whether it serves a broad need shared by all consumers.

Retail sectors are becoming more concentrated and increasingly dominated by a handful of large, multiple-location chain stores, warehouse clubs, home centers, and supercenters. Consumers are fueling this trend by consolidating their purchases and shopping at fewer, larger stores. Large retailers have also triggered the exit of small companies that were mainstream wholesale distribution customers. Big-box retailers serving customers in different product markets frequently benchmark their strategies and performance against one another. Consequently, practices tend to migrate quickly from one retailer to another.

Thus, wholesaler-distributors serving retail markets face a shrinking number of potential customers even as overall retail sales continue to expand. Exhibit 8-2 shows the 10 retail subsegments with the highest and lowest net change in number of stores through 2004. The biggest change was a format shift away from traditional gas stations to combination gas stations and convenience stores, which resulted in 5,800 net fewer gas stations. Other sectors face changing consumer preferences. Florists now sell less than one-half of all flowers purchased in the United States because supermarkets have added a floral category and Internet florists have captured a small but growing portion of the market. Specialty clothing stores are being replaced by larger, multiple-category general merchandise superstores.

Regardless of the reason, the loss of a viable customer base will challenge wholesaler-distributors. One executive at a floral products wholesaler told us: "Our company has approximately 1,500 customers that we serve weekly. In the past 6 months, 68 of these traditional retailers have gone out of business."

Exhibit 8-1. U.S. retail sales by type of store.

Type of Store	2005 Annual Retail Sales (billions)	Number of Stores	Average Sales Per Store (millions)
Motor Vehicle and Parts Dealers	$895.3	128,000	$7.0
Food and Beverage Stores	$519.3	153,000	$3.4
General Merchandise Stores	$525.7	44,000	$11.9
Foodservices and Drinking Places	$396.6	529,000	$0.7
Building Materials and Garden Equipment Dealers	$327.0	87,000	$3.8
Gasoline Stations	$388.3	118,000	$3.3
Nonstore Retailers (Catalog and Internet)	$249.0	n.a.	n.a.
Health and Personal Care Stores	$208.4	84,000	$2.5
Clothing and Clothing Accessories Stores	$201.7	150,000	$1.3
Miscellaneous Store Retailers	$111.0	129,000	$0.9
Furniture and Home Furnishing Stores	$111.3	66,000	$1.7
Electronics and Appliance Stores	$100.4	49,000	$2.0
Sporting Goods, Hobby, Book, and Music Stores	$81.9	62,000	$1.3
Total	**$4,115.8**	**1,599,000**	**$2.6**

Source: U.S. Census Bureau

Exhibit 8-2. Change in number of retail stores.

Type of Store	Number of Stores, 2004	Net Change, 1998 to 2004	Percent Change, 1998 to 2004
MOST STORES GAINED			
Gasoline Stations with Convenience Stores	92,611	10,427	13%
General Merchandise Stores	31,787	7,363	30%
Appliance, Television, and Other Electronics Stores	35,487	6,670	23%
Specialty Food Stores	15,682	3,682	31%
Other Home Furnishings Stores	21,965	3,227	17%
MOST STORES LOST			
Gasoline Stations	25,476	-16,234	-39%
Building Materials Dealers	38,152	-5,601	-13%
Florists	21,667	-3,950	-15%
Women's Clothing Stores	33,791	-3,651	-10%
Men's Clothing Stores	8,758	-3,103	-26%

Source: Pembroke Consulting analysis of U.S. Census Bureau data

THE ROLE OF WHOLESALE DISTRIBUTION

Total wholesale distribution revenues for many lines of trade serving the retail market are still quite high. (See Exhibit 8-3). However, the role and function of wholesale distribution is changing in many of these subsectors.

Smaller retail customers rely on wholesalers for direct delivery to an individual store location. In contrast, most large chain retailers act as their own wholesaler because they have developed self-warehousing capabilities for distributing products to individual stores from the retailer's own warehouses. Retail chains have the volume to economically substitute direct-store delivery by a wholesaler for self-warehousing and redistribution using their own facilities.

For example, grocery wholesaling, which represents 11% of total wholesale distribution industry revenues, faces shrinking capacity utilization as larger retailers bypass the traditional channel. This sector represented more than 15% of total wholesale distribution industry revenues in 1992, but has been a shrinking part of the industry since at least that time.

Self-distributing retail chains, such as Safeway and Kroger, and also Wal-Mart, have transformed the wholesale grocery industry. Retail consolidation has replaced small *mom-and-pop* grocery stores with a handful of professionally managed, publicly traded retailers that have national scope. Wal-Mart, which has a more than 20% share of U.S. retail grocery sales, is accelerating the shakeout among smaller chains, which are another traditional wholesale distribution customer group. Real (inflation-adjusted) revenues of grocery wholesalers have been essentially flat since 2001.

In contrast, sales at restaurants and bars continue to grow faster than grocery sales, reflecting a long-term shift away from home cooking. Foodservice supplies distributors have a more stable role in the channel because the majority of restaurants are still single location operations. Institutional customers, such as hospitals, school districts, and prisons, often rely on a wholesale distribution intermediary because food is not these customers' primary function.

Purchases from wholesaler-distributors are expected to trend downward faster than in other markets. (See Exhibit 8-4.) As noted above, many large retailers bypass wholesaler-distributors and purchase directly from manufacturers. However, the fact that an unusually high 60% of sales will still flow through wholesale distribution in our data reflects two factors. First, the mix of wholesale distribution executives available to participate in this study is naturally skewed toward industries in which wholesale distribution still plays a role. Second, some larger wholesalers leverage their own buying power, information systems, and geographic coverage to maintain a role by delivering to the warehouses of large retailers. We consider the second factor in the next section where we discuss the fee-for-service logistics trend.

Purchases from other retailers are a significant factor in retail markets, representing 12% of channel sales in 2006 and forecast to decline only slightly in the next 5 years. Large supercenters and warehouse clubs sometimes sell products below the prices paid by wholesale distribution companies and typically open earlier and close later than wholesaler-distributors. The NAW/DREF study *Competing for Customers: How Wholesaler-Distributors Can Meet the Power Retailer Challenge,* published when these clubs were first gaining prominence in the mid 1990s, found that 74% of small retailers had purchased something from a warehouse club.[32] Restaurants were most likely to have purchased from a club (86%), followed by grocery stores (76%), sporting goods stores (71%), and auto parts stores (70%).

Exhibit 8-3. Total wholesaler-distributor revenues in selected lines of trade.

Line of Trade (defined by primary products)	Total Wholesaler-Distributor Revenues* (billions)	Share of Revenue by Market				
		Building Materials and Contractor Supplies	MRO Supplies (Industrial and Commercial)	OEM and Production Materials	Retail Stores and Dealers	Export Sales
Grocery and Foodservice Wholesaler-Distributors	$434.1	0%	4%	3%	90%	4%
Oil and Gas Products Wholesaler-Distributors	$392.1	4%	23%	14%	52%	8%
Automotive and Other Vehicles Aftermarket Parts	$311.1	2%	20%	7%	69%	2%
Full-Line Pharmaceutical Wholesalers	$263.3	0%	0%	0%	99%	1%
Apparel and Piece Goods Wholesaler-Distributors	$120.3	0%	4%	5%	89%	3%
Beer, Wine, and Liquor Wholesalers	$96.9	0%	0%	0%	99%	1%
Computer and Peripheral Equipment for Resale	$94.3	0%	3%	0%	85%	12%
Tobacco and Tobacco Products	$72.5	0%	0%	0%	99%	0%
Furniture and Home Furnishings	$64.3	8%	5%	1%	63%	1%
Household Appliances	$58.0	3%	11%	2%	78%	7%
Diamonds, Jewelry, and Precious Stones/Metals	$42.8	0%	1%	12%	84%	4%

Share of Revenue by Market

Line of Trade (defined by primary products)	Total Wholesaler-Distributor Revenues* (billions)	Building Materials and Contractor Supplies	MRO Supplies (Industrial and Commercial)	OEM and Production Materials	Retail Stores and Dealers	Export Sales
Books, Periodicals, and Newspapers	$30.5	0%	4%	0%	94%	2%
Sporting and Recreational Goods and Supplies	$26.6	6%	5%	1%	85%	4%
Toy and Hobby Goods and Supplies	$24.4	0%	0%	0%	100%	0%
Prerecorded Media (CDs, DVDs, and Videotapes)	$14.8	0%	7%	1%	89%	3%
Flowers and Floral Supplies	$12.8	4%	2%	3%	90%	2%
Photographic Equipment and Supplies	$11.9	0%	0%	0%	100%	0%
Restaurant/Hotel Equipment and Supplies	$11.8	4%	9%	0%	85%	1%
Art Goods and Novelties	$10.8	0%	9%	0%	89%	1%
Optical and Ophthalmic Goods	$6.2	0%	11%	1%	86%	3%
Musical Instruments and Supplies	$2.8	0%	2%	0%	88%	10%

*July 2005 through June 2006

Figures do not add to 100% due to rounding.

Source: 2006 Wholesale Distribution Economic Reports. Latest data are available in 2007 Wholesale Distribution Economic Reports at www.nawpubs.org.

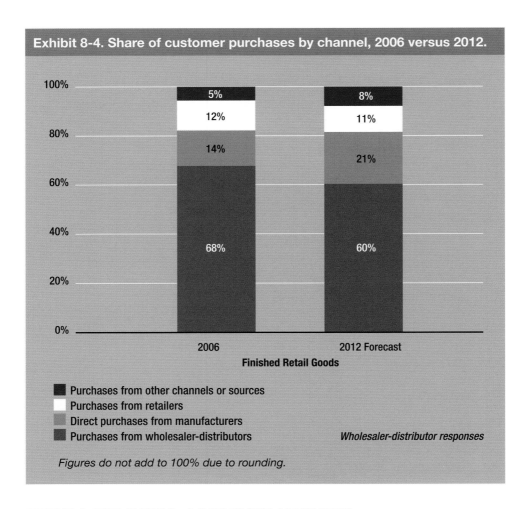

Exhibit 8-4. Share of customer purchases by channel, 2006 versus 2012.

Finished Retail Goods

- ■ Purchases from other channels or sources
- □ Purchases from retailers
- ▨ Direct purchases from manufacturers
- ■ Purchases from wholesaler-distributors

Wholesaler-distributor responses

Figures do not add to 100% due to rounding.

TRENDS FOR RETAIL CONSUMER MARKETS

Trend 1: Private Label Products

More than one-half of wholesaler-distributors in retail markets offer their private label products, and this is more than any other group except OEM and production materials. (See Exhibit 8-5.)

Many wholesaler-distributors will adopt a strategy of helping small retailers compete against the retail giants. These wholesaler-distributors give independents some of the purchasing and private label advantages that large chains enjoy, such as distinctive products with the wholesaler's brand name. (See the Do it Best Corp. example in Chapter One.) These products are available only with a marketing program, co-op, or franchise relationship.

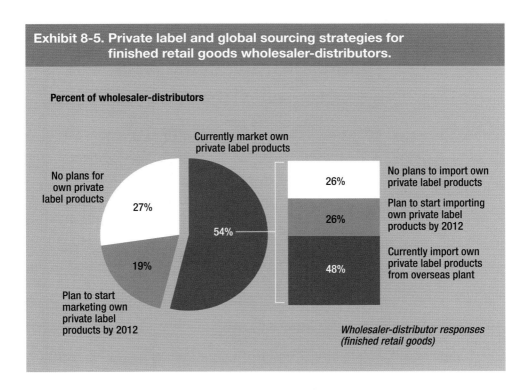

Exhibit 8-5. Private label and global sourcing strategies for finished retail goods wholesaler-distributors.

Percent of wholesaler-distributors

Currently market own private label products

No plans for own private label products

27%

54%

19%

Plan to start marketing own private label products by 2012

No plans to import own private label products — 26%

Plan to start importing own private label products by 2012 — 26%

Currently import own private label products from overseas plant — 48%

Wholesaler-distributor responses (finished retail goods)

Trend 2: Demand-Driven Channels

As described in Chapter Two, the demand-driven concept originated in retail industries. Mass merchandisers and big-box retailers expect manufacturers to use VMI to restock inventory based on actual sales. This trend diminishes the role of distributors by more closely integrating manufacturer-retailer relations. As a result, wholesaler-distributors in our study see retail customers increasing their direct purchasing from manufacturers over the next 5 years. (See Exhibit 8-4.)

Wholesaler-distributors in retail markets share data with more suppliers than in other markets. (See Exhibit 8-6.) The percentage of wholesaler-distributors that didn't share point-of-sale data with their suppliers (39%) in 2006 is similar to other markets. However, 47% did share data with six or more suppliers and this figure is substantially higher than in other markets. Similarly, the percent expecting not to share point-of-sale data in 2012 is similar to other markets, but the number of suppliers is higher than in other markets.

About one-third of wholesaler-distributors in retail markets have VMI agreements with customers, and this figure is expected to more than double to 73% of wholesaler-distributors by 2012. (See Exhibit 2-3.) Some wholesalers extend the demand-driven concept even further and work on consigned inventory programs

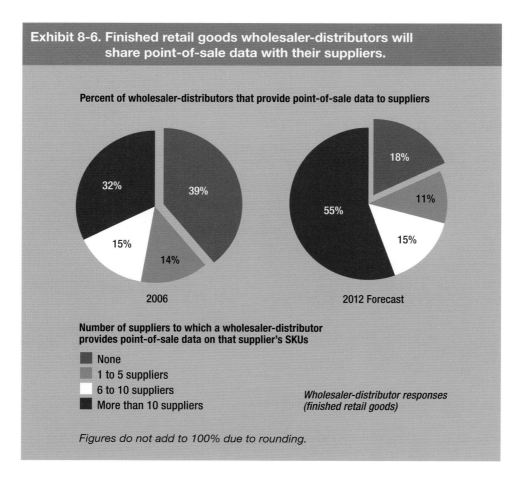

Exhibit 8-6. Finished retail goods wholesaler-distributors will share point-of-sale data with their suppliers.

Percent of wholesaler-distributors that provide point-of-sale data to suppliers

2006

2012 Forecast

Number of suppliers to which a wholesaler-distributor provides point-of-sale data on that supplier's SKUs

- None
- 1 to 5 suppliers
- 6 to 10 suppliers
- More than 10 suppliers

Wholesaler-distributor responses (finished retail goods)

Figures do not add to 100% due to rounding.

with major customers. In this situation, the wholesaler owns the inventory that sits on the shelves of a retail store's establishments. Using scan-based technology, wholesalers get paid only after the product is sold to a household consumer. The retailer only takes title of the inventory for a brief time while the ownership is transferred to the end customer. As part of a consigned inventory agreement, the wholesaler-distributor supplies products as needed, while the retailer postpones the costs of owning the inventory and reduces inventory management and storage costs.

Trend 3: New Profit Models

Similar to other markets, wholesaler-distributors in retail markets expect that manufacturers will take on more responsibility for a wholesaler-distributor's profit margin from product distribution. (See Exhibit 8-7.)

One significant difference is the comparatively low-percentage increase in fee-for-service payments from customers versus other markets. (See Exhibits 6-9 and 7-9.)

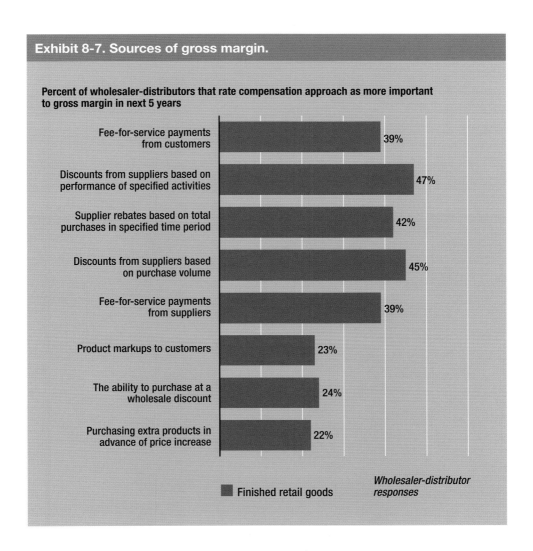

Exhibit 8-7. Sources of gross margin.

Percent of wholesaler-distributors that rate compensation approach as more important to gross margin in next 5 years

Fee-for-service payments from customers	39%
Discounts from suppliers based on performance of specified activities	47%
Supplier rebates based on total purchases in specified time period	42%
Discounts from suppliers based on purchase volume	45%
Fee-for-service payments from suppliers	39%
Product markups to customers	23%
The ability to purchase at a wholesale discount	24%
Purchasing extra products in advance of price increase	22%

■ Finished retail goods

Wholesaler-distributor responses

It is important to remember that retail customers are also distribution channels. As a result, wholesaler-distributors often have fewer opportunities to offer value-added services related to product knowledge and are limited to providing inventory and availability to retailers.

This shift to supplier compensation also reflects the greater bargaining power of volume retailers. (See Exhibit 3-1.) As we discuss above, retail chains can credibly threaten to bypass wholesale distribution for self-warehousing and redistribution using their own facilities.

Fee-for-service logistics will be an important component of compensation, especially for large wholesaler-distributors in retail markets. Some wholesaler-distributors have sustained a role in highly consolidated retail channels by delivering products to customers' warehouses. Warehouse shipments do not typically generate substantial traditional markup product margins because the wholesaler's role is reduced to pure logistics and fulfillment.

About 66% of wholesaler-distributors in retail markets expect to offer logistics as a fee-based service. This amount is slightly more than some companies in other markets. (See Exhibit 3-5.) The perceived competitive threat from logistics companies has not increased substantially in the 3 years since the last report. (See Exhibit 8-8.) New developments, such as the Imperial Tobacco Canada–Ryder System example in the Action Ideas section of Chapter Three, could quickly change this assessment.

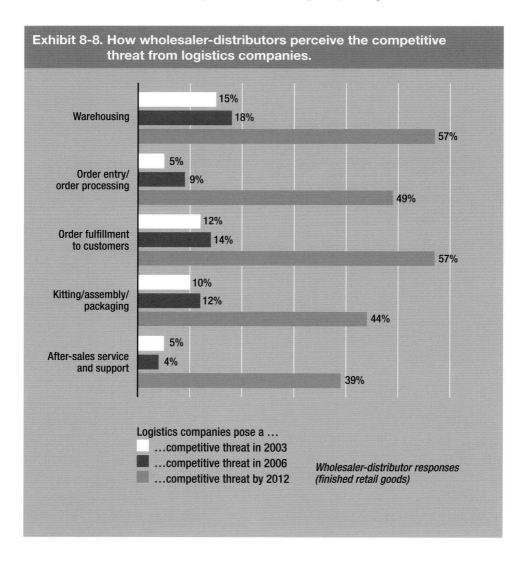

Exhibit 8-8. How wholesaler-distributors perceive the competitive threat from logistics companies.

Warehousing
- 15%
- 18%
- 57%

Order entry/order processing
- 5%
- 9%
- 49%

Order fulfillment to customers
- 12%
- 14%
- 57%

Kitting/assembly/packaging
- 10%
- 12%
- 44%

After-sales service and support
- 5%
- 4%
- 39%

Logistics companies pose a ...
- ...competitive threat in 2003
- ...competitive threat in 2006
- ...competitive threat by 2012

Wholesaler-distributor responses (finished retail goods)

Trend 4: Connected Customers

The consumer-oriented nature of retail markets means that online interactions will have significant implications for wholesaler-distributors in this market.

Online ordering will see substantial growth, while ordering methods that are still termed *traditional* in other customer segments will see a sustained decline. Mail, telephone, and fax orders continue to trend downward, as do orders placed face-to-face with a sales rep.

Although EDI has historically dominated online ordering methods for this market, orders placed on a wholesaler-distributor's Web site are catching up quickly. In our 2004 report, we found that Web orders were estimated to represent only 3% of a wholesaler-distributor's sales revenue in 2003 and forecast to grow to 13% by 2008. Consistent with that forecast, Web orders were 11% of revenue in 2006 and forecast to double to 22% by 2012. (See Exhibit 8-9.)

Exhibit 8-9. A wholesaler-distributor's sales revenue by customer ordering method, 2006 versus 2012.

	Percent of a Wholesaler-Distributor's Sales Revenue	
Finished Retail Goods	2006	2012
TRADITIONAL ORDERING METHODS		
Mail, telephone, or fax	32%	23%
Walk-in and counter sales	5%	5%
Face-to-face with sales representative	32%	25%
Subtotal	*69%*	*53%*
ONLINE ORDERING METHODS		
E-mail sent to your company	4%	7%
Online via wholesaler-distributor's Web site	11%	22%
Online via third-party Web site	2%	3%
Via Electronic Data Interchange (EDI)	14%	17%
Subtotal	*31%*	*49%*
Total	**100%**	**100%**

Wholesaler-distributor responses

Figures do not add to 100% due to rounding.

This growth reflects customer behavior in fragmented retail markets served by wholesaler-distributors. Smaller retail customers are similar in many ways to contractors. Staff does the purchasing locally. Customers deal primarily with a few suppliers that can deliver the wide range of products required within a simple and straightforward billing system. To remain viable, these businesses rely on services from their supply chain partners. To maintain these retail customers, wholesaler-distributors will have to automate to accept Web-based electronic orders. Retail buyers are likely to use the Internet for information and to find new sources of supply, so that they can stay on top of product trends. Once they see a need for a new product, they will seek out new sources of supply. In this way, they also tend to behave more like smaller contractors than larger business customers.

APPENDIX A **About This Report**

Facing the Forces of Change® is the only major research study analyzing the future of wholesale distribution within multiple supply chains. The *Facing the Forces of Change* series provides insights about the overall future of the wholesale distribution industry and the role of wholesaler-distributors. The breadth and scope of the report allows us to consider similarities among the diverse lines of trade represented by NAW rather than merely highlighting a single line of trade.

- *Facing the Forces of Change®: Lead the Way in the Supply Chain* retains many elements that made our 2004 report so popular and successful, such as a straightforward presentation of major trends, management discussion questions, and detailed subgroup analyses of data. This edition also includes some important improvements.

- This is the first report in the 25-year history of *Facing the Forces of Change* that provides comparative data from a previous report; this allows us a fresh assessment of past predictions.

- This report contains twice as many examples as in the 2004 edition, allowing us to illustrate the trends with many specific industries and companies. The report's specific examples will help all wholesale distribution executives develop new strategies for innovating in the supply chain.

- We have integrated findings about the channel management plans of suppliers into the trend discussions rather than including them in a separate chapter. This change will help wholesale distribution executives better anticipate future supplier strategies.

- As described in the Introduction, we have modified the classification system introduced in the 2004 report to correspond more closely to traditional wholesale distribution industry descriptions.

This report integrates a broad set of information ranging from opinions of executives to extensive external and objective data from outside the wholesale distribution industry.

- This report includes in-depth interviews with wholesale distribution executives, manufacturers, customers, consultants, financial analysts, professors, and trade association executives. These interviews ensured that we obtained a broad perspective on the future trends.

- Nearly 1,000 survey responses from wholesale distribution executives in 73 NAW member associations were received. More than one-half of these individuals also provided additional information via three supplemental surveys conducted after the original survey. Responses came from companies whose annual revenues were representative of the entire wholesale distribution industry.

- Close to 300 survey responses were received from senior executives at supply companies to wholesaler-distributors. These executives were given a different survey than wholesale distribution executives and they answered questions about their current and future channel strategies.

- We conducted extensive analyses of U.S. government data from the U.S. Census Bureau, U.S. Bureau of Labor Statistics, and U.S. Bureau of Economic Analysis.

- We conducted primary and secondary research on companies and industries, including media accounts of major issues impacting the industry or significant industry announcements.

- We conducted a review of external studies from trade associations, other consulting firms, and academic researchers.

Market Groups for NAW Member Associations

This appendix relates the major markets discussed in *Facing the Forces of Change®: Lead the Way in the Supply Chain* to NAW's member associations, which are primarily organized based on product type. This chart indicates the typical or primary markets for members of a particular association. *Please use this list as a general guideline only.* Distributors that belong to the associations shown may also participate in other markets. See Exhibits 6-2, 7-3, and 8-3 for total wholesaler-distributor revenues within the major markets.

NAW Member Association	Construction Markets	Industrial and Commercial Markets	Retail Consumer Markets
1 American Machine Tool Distributors Association	●	●	
2 American Nursery and Landscape Association	●		●
3 American Supply Association	●	●	
4 American Veterinary Distributors Association		●	
5 American Wholesale Marketers Association			●
6 Appliance Parts Distributors Association Inc.		●	●
7 Associated Equipment Distributors	●		
8 Association for High Technology Distribution		●	
9 Association of Millwork Distributors	●		●
10 Association of Pool and Spa Professionals	●	●	
11 Association of Woodworking and Furnishings Suppliers	●	●	
12 Aviation Distributors and Manufacturers Association		●	
13 Bearing Specialists Association		●	
14 Bicycle Product Suppliers Association			●
15 Canadian Association for Pharmacy Distribution Management			●
16 Canadian Institute of Plumbing and Heating	●	●	

NAW Member Association	Construction Markets	Industrial and Commercial Markets	Retail Consumer Markets
17 Ceramic Tile Distributors Association	●		
18 Cleaning Equipment Trade Association	●	●	●
19 Commercial Vehicle Solutions Network		●	●
20 Copper and Brass Servicenter Association		●	
21 Door and Hardware Institute	●		
22 Electrical Apparatus Service Association, Inc.	●	●	
23 Electro-Federation Canada Inc.	●	●	
24 Farm Equipment Wholesalers Association	●	●	
25 Fluid Power Distributors Association, Inc.	●	●	
26 Food Industry Suppliers Association		●	
27 Foodservice Equipment Distributors Association		●	●
28 Gases and Welding Distributors Association	●	●	
29 General Merchandise Distributors Council			●
30 Global Technology Distribution Council		●	
31 Health Industry Distributors Association		●	●
32 Healthcare Distribution Management Association			●

NAW Member Association	Construction Markets	Industrial and Commercial Markets	Retail Consumer Markets
33 Heating, Airconditioning and Refrigeration Distributors International	●	●	
34 Independent Distributor Association	●		●
35 Independent Sealing Distributors		●	
36 Industrial Compressor Distributor Association		●	
37 Industrial Supply Association		●	
38 International Association of Plastics Distributors	●	●	
39 International Foodservice Distributors Association			●
40 International Sanitary Supply Association	●	●	●
41 International Truck Parts Association		●	
42 Irrigation Association	●	●	
43 Lawn and Garden Marketing and Distribution Association	●		●
44 Machinery Dealers National Association	●		
45 Material Handling Equipment Distributors Association	●	●	●
46 Metals Service Center Institute		●	
47 Motorcycle Industry Council			●
48 Music Distributors Association			●

NAW Member Association	Construction Markets	Industrial and Commercial Markets	Retail Consumer Markets
49 NAHAD The Association for Hose and Accessories Distribution		●	
50 National Association of Chemical Distributors		●	
51 National Association of Electrical Distributors	●	●	
52 National Association of Flour Distributors, Inc.			●
53 National Association of Sign Supply Distributors		●	
54 National Association of Sporting Goods Wholesalers			●
55 National Association of Uniform Manufacturers and Distributors		●	
56 National Beer Wholesalers Association			●
57 National Convenience Stores Distributors Association			●
58 National Fastener Distributors Association	●	●	
59 National Grocers Association			●
60 National Insulation Association	●		
61 National Kitchen and Bath Association	●		
62 National Marine Distributors Association			●
63 National Paper Trade Association Inc.		●	
64 National School Supply and Equipment Association		●	●

NAW Member Association	Construction Markets	Industrial and Commercial Markets	Retail Consumer Markets
65 National Wood Flooring Association	●		
66 North American Association of Floor Covering Distributors	●	●	
67 North American Association of Utility Distributors	●	●	
68 North American Building Material Distribution Association	●		
69 North American Horticultural Supply Association			●
70 North American Meat Processors Association			●
71 North American Wholesale Lumber Association, Inc.	●	●	
72 NPES The Association for Suppliers of Printing, Publishing and Converting Technologies		●	●
73 Office Products Wholesalers Association			●
74 Optical Laboratories Association			●
75 Outdoor Power Equipment and Engine Service Association, Inc.	●		●
76 Outdoor Power Equipment Aftermarket Association	●		●
77 Pet Industry Distributors Association			●
78 Petroleum Equipment Institute		●	●
79 Post Card and Souvenir Distributors Association			●
80 Power Transmission Distributors Association		●	

NAW Member Association	Construction Markets	Industrial and Commercial Markets	Retail Consumer Markets
81 Professional Beauty Association			●
82 Recreational Vehicle Aftermarket Association			●
83 Safety Equipment Distributors Association, Inc.	●	●	
84 Security Hardware Distributors Association	●		●
85 Textile Care Allied Trades Association		●	●
86 United Products Formulators and Distributors Association		●	
87 Water and Sewer Distributors of America	●	●	
88 Wholesale Florist and Florist Supplier Association			●
89 Wine and Spirits Wholesalers of America, Inc.			●
90 Woodworking Machinery Industry Association	●	●	●

APPENDIX C Wholesaler-Distributor Revenues in Selected Machinery and Equipment Lines of Trade

This table shows total revenues for wholesaler-distributors of machinery and equipment products. Wholesaler-distributors of these products operate across the three major markets described in Chapters Six through Eight, although the capital equipment purchasing process differs from purchases of other durable or nondurable products. We provide this table as a supplemental reference to the data presented in Exhibits 6-2, 7-3, and 8-3.

Line of Trade (defined by primary products)	Total Wholesaler-Distributor Revenues* (billions)
Computer and Peripheral Equipment for End Use	$63.7
Industrial Machinery and Equipment	$65.9
Communications Equipment and Other Electronic Parts	$54.7
Farm and Garden Machinery and Equipment	$45.3
Construction Machinery and Equipment	$45.1
Office Equipment (excluding computers)	$31.7
Materials Handling Machinery, Equipment, and Parts	$17.7
Metalworking Machinery, Equipment, and Parts	$14.3
Fluid Power Machinery, Equipment, and Parts	$14.1
Oil Well, Refinery, and Pipeline Equipment and Supplies	$10.1
Food Processing Machinery, Equipment, and Parts	$4.5
Store Machines and Equipment	$4.3

*July 2005 through June 2006

Source: 2006 Wholesale Distribution Economic Reports. Latest data are available in 2007 Wholesale Distribution Economic Reports at www.nawpubs.org.

Endnotes

[1] Profitability data come from the U.S. Census Bureau's Quarterly Financial Reports, which included wholesaler-distributors representing approximately 42% of total wholesale distribution industry revenues in 2006.

[2] These questions are adapted from "Sharpening Your Business Acumen," Ram Charan, *Strategy + Business*, Spring 2006. Available at http://www.strategy-business.com/magazine.

[3] *The Power of Private Label 2005: A Review of Growth Trends Around the World*, AC Nielson. Available at http://www2.acnielsen.com/reports/documents/2005_privatelabel.pdf.

[4] "The Chinese Export Juggernaut in Manufactures Overtakes the United States and the Policy Implications," Ernest H. Preeg, *Manufacturers Alliance/MAPI Economic Report*, March 21, 2006.

[5] "Wal-Mart, Metro to Buy More from China," Xinhua News Agency, November 10, 2005. Available at http://www.china.org.cn/english/BAT/148279.htm.

[6] These questions are adapted from "Manage Consolidation in Your Channel," Adam J. Fein and Sandy Jap, *Sloan Management Review*, Fall 1999.

[7] *Global Supply Chain Benchmark Report*, Aberdeen Group, June 2006.

[8] "A Logistical Look at China," *Forbes*, October 2, 2006.

[9] For an overview of this research, see "On Bullwhip in Supply Chains—Historical Review, Present Practice and Expected Future Impact," *International Journal of Production Economics*, 2006.

[10] *Achieving Effective Inventory Management, Third Edition*, Jon Schreibfeder, Effective Inventory Management, Inc., 2005. Available at http://www.naw.org/aeim/.

[11] *ERP in Distribution*, chapter 9, Barry Lawrence, Daniel Jennings, and Brian Reynolds, 2005.

[12] *2005 TLI/WERC Warehousing Benchmark Report*, Edward H. Frazelle, Warehousing Education and Research Council (WERC) and The Logistics Institute (TLI), Georgia Tech University. Available at http://www.logisticsvillage.com/MediaCenter/Documents/Presentations/2005WarehouseBenchmarkingRpt.pdf.

[13] "RFID's Impact on Out of Stocks: A Sales Velocity Analysis," Bill Hardgrave, Matthew Waller, and Robert Miller, Information Technology Research Institute, Sam. M. Walton College of Business, University of Arkansas, June 4, 2006. Available at http://itrc.uark.edu/research/display.asp?article=ITRI-WP068-0606.

[14] "Reinvigorating Supplier Relationships," Mark Dancer, in *OUTLOOK 2006: An Executive's Companion to Facing the Forces of Change®*, National Association of Wholesaler-Distributors/Distribution Research and Education Foundation, 2005. Out of print.

[15] "Recommended Best Practices: Collection of Point-of-Sale (POS) or Point-of-Transfer (POT) Data," National Association of Electrical Distributors, October 27, 2005. Available at http://www.naed.org/images/Admin/POSWhitepaper.pdf.

[16] To read more about fee-for-service in the pharmaceutical supply chain, see *Challenge in the Channel: A Critical Review of the U.S. Pharmaceutical Industry*, Pembroke Consulting, March 2005. Available at http://www.pembrokeconsulting.com/ima.html, and "Drive the Right Supply Chain Behaviors," *Supply Chain Strategy*, August 2005. Available at http://harvardbusinessonline.hbsp.harvard.edu.

[17] *The 10th Annual Third-Party Logistics Study*, 2005, is available with registration at http://www.3plstudy.com.

[18] All data in this section come from the Pew Internet and American Life Project at http://www.pewinternet.org, a nonprofit research initiative that has been surveying large samples of Americans throughout the past 7 years.

[19] "The New Media Ecology: How the Internet is Changing Consumer Behavior and Expectations," Lee Rainie, Pew Internet and American Life Project, May 9, 2006. Available at http://www.pewinternet.org/ppt/2006%20-%205.9.06%20SOCAP.pdf.

[20] "Industrial Marketing Online: Getting Industrial Buyers and Sellers on the Same Page," ThomasNet.com. Available at http://www.thomasnet.com/pressroom/whitepapers.html.

[21] General information on forums comes from the "Internet Forums" listing in Wikipedia at http://en.wikipedia.org/wiki/Internet_forum.

[22] *2006 E-Business Trends in Manufacturing Report*, SVM E-Business Solutions, February 2006. Available at http://www.svmsolutions.com/survey/.

[23] "May I help you?", *INC. magazine*, January 2006.

[24] "B2B E-mail Marketing Best Practices: Hewlett-Packard," Forrester Research, February 21, 2006. Available at http://jobfunctions.bnet.com/abstract.aspx?promo=50002anddocid=167459.

[25] *Consolidation in Wholesale Distribution: Understanding Industry Change*, National Association of Wholesaler-Distributors/Distribution Research and Education Foundation, 1997. Out of print.

[26] *2006 Wholesale Distribution Economic Reports*, National Association of Wholesaler-Distributors. Out of print. Latest data are available in *2007 Wholesale Distribution Economic Reports*. Available at www.nawpubs.org.

[27] *The 21st Century at Work: Forces Shaping the Future Workforce and Workplace in the United States*, Lynn A. Karoly and Constantijn W.A. Panis, RAND Corporation, 2004. Available at www.rand.org.

[28] Portions of this section are adapted from Pembroke Consulting's independent research 2006 study *Closing the Growth Gap*, which was sponsored by Lawson Software (www.lawson.com). The complete report is available for free download at www.lawson.com/dis_growth.

[29] *The State of the Nation's Housing 2006*, Joint Center for Housing Studies of Harvard University. Available at http://www.jchs.harvard.edu/publications/markets/son2006.

[30] *The 60th Annual Survey of Distributor Operations, Industrial Distribution* and Reed Business Information, 2006. Available at http://idmag.stores.yahoo.net/60ansuofdiop.html.

[31] *2005 Skills Gap Report: A Survey of the American Manufacturing Workforce*, National Association of Manufacturers. Available at www.nam.org.

[32] *Competing for Customers: How Wholesaler-Distributors Can Meet the Power Retailer Challenge*, National Association of Wholesaler-Distributors/Distribution Research and Education Foundation, 1995. Out of print.